Canoe Building

Canoe Building

in glass reinforced plastic

Alan Byde

ADAM & CHARLES BLACK
LONDON

First published 1974

A & C Black Limited
4, 5 & 6 Soho Square, London W1V 6AD

© 1974 Alan W Byde

ISBN 0 7136 1457 9

Printed in Great Britain by
Bristol Typesetting Co. Ltd
Barton Manor St Philips Bristol

Contents

List of Drawings

List of Drawings

Preface

Graham sat on the quay-side. His only plimsoll squelched wetly as he wiggled his toes. The canoe lay broken-backed beside him. Two well-built fishermen who manned the inshore rescue craft which had rescued him went grimly about the business of putting away the inflatable craft. Ten minutes later the Land-Rover found him and the shattered canoe was tied on the roof. Later in camp the remains were put on the trailer for rebuilding back at the Youth Centre where it had been made.

That canoe was almost new. It had done four hard days on a river then a day surfing, then a day out to some islands. The coastguard had watched it go out, and when it was obviously sinking, he watched with greater care. Suddenly, through the telescope, he saw it roll over. What he didn't see, as he called out the rescue service, and had a helicopter on stand-by, was the group calmly rescuing the waterlogged boat, emptying it, and carrying on with the trip. He was embarrassed later, but as he said, you can't tell an expert group from a bunch of beginners, not a mile away. It sank again, on the surf line, beside the rescue boat, and the fishermen broke the back of the boat as they hauled it, heavy with water, into their rescue boat.

Why did the canoe take in water? The builder had made a poor joint between deck and hull, and that part behind the cockpit on the right side had opened up for about eighteen inches. Water constantly slopped in as the flexible top and bottom of the canoe bent under the lift of the waves passing. That was the first boat he had ever built. He always made excellent joints after that.

Cautionary tale ends. It did happen, in August 1968 in Northumberland.

This book has had a long and difficult birth. The influences are many. In 1966 it was a duplicated five-page handout done for schools and friends; it became a booklet by Trylon now in its third edition. Part of it was a chapter in *Living Canoeing* and is now another chapter in *Canoeing Complete*, third edition. It first 'brewed' in a cricket pavilion at Durham School, unheated, in the hard winter of 1962-3, when resin took seven days to set; it developed through a Wolverhampton school, and then Riverside Centre, Oxford. There were week-end forays to Scotland, Sussex, South Wales and North London over seven years, during which hundreds of canoes were built. In 1971 at Llangollen, John Crane from Trylon, John Earle from the BBC and I, plus a TV production and technical crew of around sixty people, got together and recorded two twenty-five minute programmes in the series called *Canoe* which appeared on BBC 1 in 1972—three times. It was repeated for the fourth time in March 1973. It was said that the response to the canoe-building programme was over 7,000 in the first four weeks. The book simply had to be written. It has been criticised by a vet, a car production worker, a highly qualified expert in gas chromatography, and a lecturer in house-building techniques. They all have one thing in common; they have all built their own canoes, and they canoe for enjoyment.

The book is written by one who has made many mistakes in canoe building, and in using glass-reinforced plastics. No apologies are made for writing as an amateur; I do it because I love it. The craftsman will call the enthusiastic amateur the 'bodger'. Well, this is the bodger's book, based on hard experience and on what is known to be good practice. Many practical tips are offered, one or two proved methods of building canoes, and a glossary of terms which should help the absolute beginner in canoe building to begin to talk knowledgeably about the business.

As in all things worth doing there are many ways of doing them. The methods described are good basic ways of canoe building. Different ways exist, so if what is written here does not tie in with your experience so far, reject neither one nor the other as faulty, but accept both, learn both, then use that which best suits your needs.

My basic experience was on grp canoe hulls with plywood decks, then on various grp canoes and involvement with several education authorities all over Britain. Latterly, a well-equipped canoe-building workshop which is part of the Riverside Centre at Oxford has been developed and it is out of this recent development that most of this work has grown. In this workshop Centre members build canoes for themselves, for the Riverside club and for schools in the area. For example, 130 canoes were built in 1972. That adds up to a great deal of experience. Take it, use it, and improve your experience.

As an author I see myself as a burning glass; the light is concentrated by it, but the energy comes from elsewhere. To those sources, some identifiable, some so remote no one can trace them; to Dave Holmes, Ian Young, Courtenay Phillips and Eric Swale; and to my wife Joan who tolerates rather well a husband who smells of styrene fumes, is prickly with glass fibres, and who keeps odd hours dictated by the needs of setting resin; to all these and to the publishers who put it before you: thank you.

If you would like specific advice on canoe building or designing, please write to me through the publishers, and enclose a stamped addressed envelope for a reply. Sometimes replies require drawings, so a minimum size of envelope 9″ by 4″ is best. The address is Alan W Byde, c/o A & C Black Ltd, 4, 5 & 6 Soho Square, London W1V 6AD.

Introduction

Every canoeist comes to canoeing this way; he sees the canoe, then carries it to the water, then he uses it. This leads to the following basic rules about the approach to canoeing:
1 The canoe shall look good
2 The canoe shall be light enough to carry
3 The canoe shall handle well, and be strong enough.

To look well it must be polished with glinting highlights, a glowing colour and a pleasing shape. The weight should be less than forty pounds for an adult and under twenty-five pounds for a twelve-year-old. The design must be sound, and suitable for the purpose. The method of construction can lend strength where it is needed without making the canoe a heavy one. Handling qualities are dependent on design, and this is not the purpose of this book. This book is about how to make a canoe in grp.

Grp means glass-reinforced plastic. The glass is in strands or fibrils, each being 1½ thousandths of a millimetre thick; the glass is made up as a bonded mat or a woven cloth. The plastic is normally a polyester resin which remains liquid until a hardener is mixed with it. When the resin and the glass are laid into a mould, as this book describes in detail, and the resin hardens, then the resulting laminate of glass fibres and hard plastic is tough, resilient and hard wearing. It is commonly known as glass-fibre (the term 'Fibreglass' is a trade name). It is preferable to refer to this material as grp.

Stages in canoe building

A glass-reinforced plastic canoe has gone through several well-defined stages. These are as follows:

1 The experience
2 The idea
3 The drawings
4 The plug (or pattern)
5 The moulds
6 The canoe
7 The criticism
8 The improvement
9 New mould
10 New canoe
11 Fresh criticism.

Most of the readers of this book will be interested in stages 5 and 6, but an indication of the rest of the work necessary will be useful and is included.

Glossary of terms

The following words and their meanings are both in correct English and in slang terms. Some of the latter are very expressive and are commonly used in grp workshops, and each job has its terms which one must master before full understanding can be achieved.

One term which is constantly used is grp which means glass-reinforced plastic. Some people call the material glass-fibre, which is permissible, but the term 'Fibreglass' is a trade name, and could be confusing (see page 11).

Accelerator, a blue-coloured liquid, a cobalt soap. Not so much used now that pre-accelerated resins are available. Sometimes called promoter. Increases rate at which resin and catalyst react and so reduces setting time. If kept in a polythene bottle in any light, will become a leathery solid.

Acetone. See **Cleaner brush.**

Armature, the rough unsmoothed heart of the first plug. It simply makes up a shape near enough to the required final shape, always slightly smaller, to allow for filling to the required size. Not a term that is used very often.

Bagging. When glass mat is wetted out the strands of glass no longer adhere to each other, as the binder has softened completely and has absorbed the wet resin. The strands now can slide apart a little and if wet mat is hanging from something rather than laying on something, it will go baggy. After that, no matter what one does, the material can only stretch more

14

and more. In these circumstances it is necessary to bind it up with glass cloth.

Barrier cream, a skin-protecting cream which is rubbed in on hands and forearms, but *not* the face; the cream can sting soft skin. Essential for skin care, very necessary when working with young people.

Binder, glass mat, the resin dressing on glass mat which keeps the strands together.

Birds' nest, lumps in glass mat, caused by bunching of the fibres.

Bolster, a wide-bladed bricklayer's chisel with a short steel shaft. The blade is about 4″ wide and the shaft about 8″ long. The edge of the tool should be slightly rounded off for the purpose of grp mould separation.

Brush cleaner. See **Cleaner, brush.**

Cast. The process of laying up a canoe or any object in grp is a simple casting process. The part made, e.g. the deck or hull or cockpit may be called the cast.

Catalyst, a powerful oxidising agent, usually Methyl Ethyl Ketone Peroxide (MEKP), which initiates the hardening of the resin.

Cellophane, a proprietary name for a sheet of fine transparent material. It is not attacked by resin, unlike polythene sheet which is attacked by resin and which will affect the setting of the resin. Cellophane is quite cheap.

Cheese. A cheese of rovings is barrel-shaped, very like a cheese or a roll of baler twine. The continuous strand of roving is pulled out of the centre of the cheese. Keep the cheese in its box, and pull the roving out of a suitable small hole in the top, like a ball of string.

Chopped strand mat. See under **Glass.**

Cleaner, brush. This takes several forms, but is basically acetone. It has a low flash point, and burns like petrol with a thick black smoke and a filthy stench.

Cleaner, mould, is a very fine abrasive paste, like jeweller's rouge. It is smeared on with a hand cloth, then rubbed into the surface where it cuts off the wax surface. When it is dry, it is buffed with a polishing mop turning at about 2,000 rpm.

Cloth, glass. See under **Glass.**

15

Dry lay-up. See under **Pre-wetting.**

Epoxy resin, a special resin sometimes used in canoe building. It does not attack polystyrene foam. It is of high quality, but awkward to use, and expensive. I never use it.

Exotherm. Heat generated in setting resin during its green stage.

Fence. When making a split mould, it is necessary to split the cast fore and aft. For example, on a canoe deck around the cockpit when the rim is still attached to the cockpit, it is clear that the moulding cannot be lifted off over the cockpit rim; to split the cast a small fence of alloy sheet, or even of clay, is placed where the split is required on the mould or cast, and the first half is moulded up to that. The temporary fence is then removed and the second half of the mould is made up to the flange on the first half.

Fibreglass. See introductory paragraph to Glossary.

Filler, can be almost anything, such as putty, Plasticine, clay, lead, lumps of coke (I've used it), but what is usually meant is a proprietary make of resin-based quick-setting filler. The best for most purposes is David's Isopon P 38 in 4 kilo cans. The filler fills in small holes or depressions in the surface of a plug, and can be used in many other ways in the grp workshop.

Flange, usually a flat-surfaced rim, collar or rib. It is the sort of thing one sees on old-fashioned iron piping where two lengths of pipe are bolted together. It usually runs with its plane at right angles to the surface of the mould of which it is part.

Former, gives the form or shape to the plug. It establishes the cross-section at any point. It is usually found at one-foot intervals in a plug and supports the inside of the surface of the plug.

Furane, the trade name of a type of resin which is used for putting a high-quality surface finish on a plug. The resin is mixed 1:10 catalyst and resin, and then painted on to the surface. After 30 minutes it has dried and another coat may be applied. However the surface cannot be polished or worked on until 24 hours have passed and the resin has set hard.

Gelcoat resin, a thixotropic resin, i.e. it stays where it is put. Laminating resin will tend to drain off if used as a gelcoat. Gel-

coat costs about half as much again as laminating resin. It supplies the hard outer skin of the canoe.

Glass, any form of glass fibre used to reinforce synthetic
resins.

Glass, chopped strand mat, consists of short, 3″ or 4″ strands
of glass. The strands are bonded into a mat of even thickness
by a powder binding resin. Each strand of glass may contain 80
or more fibrils of glass. Each fibril of glass is $1\frac{1}{2}$ thousandths of
a millimetre thick.

Glass cloth, a tightly woven material which is very difficult
to wet through and requires careful work to gain maximum
benefit. Some people, myself included, call woven rovings
'cloth' as a form of shorthand, but it is inaccurate.

Glass rovings, the original condition of all glass mat or cloth
or woven material. An endless 'string' of glass fibres, or rovings, is rolled on to a 6 lb 'cheese' which is then used to feed
the cutters which produce the chopped strands for chopped
strand mat, or which is woven into the warp and weft of woven
material.

Glass tissue, a very fine glass mat, almost. It looks like a
dense cobweb, and is used to bind a mat surface, or to hold
pre-wetted mat together as it is moulded into place.

Glass, woven rovings, what we erroneously call cloth. The
weave is looser than cloth, and it is easy to wet out and to remove the air.

Glass-fibre. See introductory paragraph to Glossary.

Going off, a slang term to indicate that resin is beginning to
gel, cure, or go solid. It shows by the resin looking stringy and
hanging off the brush in festoons of stringiness. The next stage
is pebble-like lumps in the resin, and then very quickly it becomes a jelly-like solid which soon starts to become warm and
then hot, and it may even start smoking.

Green life, the period when the resin has ceased to be liquid
but is not yet fully hard, and can still be cut easily.

Grp, glass-reinforced plastic. See introductory paragraph to
Glossary.

Gunge, a slang word meaning a messy liquid. It is usually
the first of the cleaning pots into which one puts the brushes
and tools for their first stage of cleaning.

Canoe Building

Laminating, the process by which a cast is built up from layers of mat or cloth. It is simply a building up of layers of material, the whole bonded together by the set resin.

Lay-up, the process of laminating, used as an alternative word to describe the process as one layer is laid up on another. Laminators talk of a 1-oz lay-up, or a $4\frac{1}{2}$-oz lay-up, thus indicating the weight of glass used in each square foot of the finished cast. A 3-oz lay-up is usual in canoe hulls.

Lay-on. When one has placed the glass mat or cloth on the mould ready for laminating the resin is then 'laid-on' with a brush or roller.

Mat. See **Chopped strand mat,** under **Glass.**

Mould, the shape into which one puts the resin and glass to obtain the required shape.

Mould cleaner. See **Cleaner, mould.**

Mould wax, usually a natural wax, *not* a silicone wax, which is used to give the surface of the mould a high degree of polish, and thus allow the cast to separate from the mould when finished.

Pebble dash surface, the rough surface caused by resin being used after it has begun to set and has gone 'crumby'.

Plug, the first shape from which the first moulds are made. It could be called the pattern, but grp practice is to call it the plug.

Polyester resin, a type of man-made resin, thus distinguished from several other types of resin systems. An ester is a product of a chemical reaction between an organic acid and an alcohol. The polyester is formed by a reaction between dibasic acids and glycol or dihydric alcohol. Most commercial polyester resins are supplied as solutions of polyester dissolved in monomeric styrene. A large number of acids, glycols, monomers, inhibitors and modifying acids are used in the production of polyester resins (one of them is called Hexachloroendomethyl-enetetrahydrophthalic acid).

Polypropylene, a synthetic material which is most useful in canoeing when made into lines for deck loops, painters etc. It is tough and hard-wearing under friction, cheap compared with nylon or terylene, and it floats, being less dense than water.

Polystyrene, a plastic which comes in solid and in foam. It is

18

attacked by polyester resin, so it must be masked off if used in a canoe. See buoyancy block fitting (page 87).

Polythene, the common material used for all kinds of household implements, and sheeting for bags and so on. It has all kinds of uses in canoe building. It is attacked by resin but not significantly.

Polyurethane. This is found in many forms, including pre-cast foam, and two-part resin which is mixed to provide an *in situ* foam mix. This is very useful for some forms of canoe building. Polyester resin does not attack it. Polyurethane paints are either one-part or two-part. These are now well-known, and useful for paddle blades etc.

Pot life. The resin is mixed in the pot, and as soon as the catalyst is stirred in, curing begins. After about 20-45 minutes the resin will cease to be liquid, but it will be not quite hard, it will be 'green'. The time that the resin remains liquid is its pot life, and should be as long as possible for inexperienced builders.

Pre-wetting. Usually one lays the resin into the mould, then lays in the glass mat or cloth, then rolls on more resin. In pre-wetting, however, the pieces of glass are laid on a wetting-out board (a piece of cardboard will do), and the resin is quickly brushed on. The stiff (but now softening) piece of glass is quickly laid into the job where required. Speed is essential, as the resin softens the glass binder in about one minute.

Promoter. See **Accelerator.**

PVA. See **Release agent.**

Registration, keeping the edges of the deck cast and the hull cast in line when joining. If the moulds are out of register, a lip or edge will be left after the two halves have been joined together. As the cast thickness is not more than $\frac{3}{32}''$, an error in register of as little as $\frac{1}{64}''$ will show up. As moulds become older and much used the flanges warp and the bolt holes become worn and the bolts loose, thus allowing the two halves of the mould to go out of register.

Release agent, a polyvinyl alcohol-based gum. It is soluble in an alcohol and when this dries out, a thin water-soluble gum is left in contact with the mould surface, which stops the resin from attacking the mould as the cast is laid inside it. After the

19

cast is made and removed it is washed and the thin skin, sometimes called 'separator', is washed off.

Resin. See **Polyester resin.** A resin is a syrup-like liquid, which becomes hard when catalyst is added. It can be had in various degrees of viscosity, and is used for various purposes. Canoe building resins are water-resisting, usually described as all-purpose resin.

Rocker. Take an average canoe and lay it on a flat hard surface, right way up. Assuming the surface to be truly flat, the centre of the canoe will rest on the ground and the ends will rise up away from the centre. The more rise, the greater the degree of rocker. Take a heavily rockered slalom kayak, and push down one end and release it. The boat will rock, like a long-based rocking-chair.

Rovings. See under **Glass.**

Stiffener. When working with such thin laminates as are usual in canoe building, large areas of flat surface, say two or three square feet, will buckle and warp quite easily. On slalom kayaks with fairly flat bottoms, these will vibrate when running fast over water as in surf or white water. The vibration of such a thin laminate is quite pronounced. Therefore it is usual to build in stiffeners to reduce the flexibility of fairly flat areas or of very thin (1 oz) laminates. The stiffeners can either be pre-formed grp ribs which are then laminated into the hull or deck, or they can be thin strips of wood.

Tissue. See under **Glass.**

Wax. Natural wax forms a highly polished skin on the mould surface, but this takes time. Do not use a silicone wax, as the resin will link with the wax, absorb it, and so stick directly to the mould.

Wetting out. As the resin and the glass are put together, the resin starts to attack the resin binder on the glass. The resin quite quickly soaks through the glass, and this is called wetting through. However, as the resin remains liquid and active, it surrounds each of the glass strands more and more intimately, and as the air bubbles are rolled out, the final cast is thoroughly wetted out. Wetting through takes five minutes, wetting out takes fifteen minutes, approximately.

Woven rovings. See under **Glass.**

20

Chapter 1

Glass and resin

Glass

Mat is weighed in ounces per square foot, and woven material in ounces per square yard (although metrication now gives us grams per square metre). A roll of 10-oz woven rovings costs about $2\frac{1}{2}$ times what a roll of mat costs. A boat built of two layers of $1\frac{1}{2}$-oz mat has a 3-oz lay-up. Usual shorthand is to say of a boat built with one layer of $1\frac{1}{2}$-oz mat for the deck and one layer of $1\frac{1}{2}$-oz mat plus one layer of 10-oz woven rovings as being a '$1\frac{1}{2}$-oz deck and $2\frac{1}{2}$-oz hull'.

MAT. Chopped strand mat is the basic material for grp work. It comes in various weights, 1-, $1\frac{1}{2}$-, 2-oz. I find $1\frac{1}{2}$-oz material most useful in my situation. Some keen clubs may find 1-oz material better for top-class slalom work. Mat can come in several qualities. First grade, which should be perfect, is of even thickness right through, and clean with a firm feel—crisp might describe it. Second grade is less expensive, but can be very good. It may be tapered from one edge to the other edge, being 2-oz at one side and 1-oz at the other, which makes good laminating difficult. The crispness may be suspect. Job lots of scraps are made up into tea chests, and are usually swept up from the factory floor. They seem to be cheap enough, but a novice trying to use material which would task an expert's skill to use properly, will become very frustrated and unhappy. Always go for best-quality materials; it saves a lot of money in the long run, and simplifies the task of novices.

When the glass mat is made, the cutters which whirl round slicing up the rovings into short lengths sometimes start to collect a bunch of these fibres. This very quickly falls off the cutters on to the moving belt which carries the chopped strands through the binder, sprays, heaters and ironing devices which prepare the mat for rolling. These clusters of strands, or birds' nests, are thicker than the surrounding mat, and can be plucked out by hand by the operatives, leaving a small hole about 1" in diameter in the mat. The end result is that the roll of glass that you get can have a few holes in it, or a few lumps. First-grade glass should not have any birds' nests or holes, and second grade should have only a few, say five in a 70-yd length. The disadvantage in laminating is that one must either remove the birds' nests and then patch over, or patch over the hole anyway. This slows down the job. If the birds' nest is left in, it is so dense that it prevents full wetting out of the lump.

Glass mat has a resin dressing on it in order to keep the strands together. This resin accepts the wet laminating resin and this rate of acceptance is important. Dampness will affect the binder and the mat becomes soft, fluffy and bad to work with. That is another reason why cheap glass can often work out very expensive in terms of wasted material, time taken and a poor end result.

WOVEN ROVINGS. Roving is a long, one could say endless, strand of glass fibres. This is then put into a loom and woven into a cloth, using the roving as one would use cotton or wool for the warp and weft. This woven material takes two forms, either woven rovings, which is quite coarse and much more suitable for canoe building, or cloth, a much finer woven material but very difficult for amateur builders to wet-out and laminate without air bubbles. It is measured in ounces per square yard, or grams per square metre. I am accustomed to using 10-oz woven rovings, which is fractionally heavier than 1-oz mat. Metrication avoids these oddities of description.

It is of interest to note that special combinations of woven rovings and mat exist. For example 'Fabmat', a commercial description, is material which is woven on one side and mat on the other. The '18-12' material is 18-oz woven material bonded to 12-oz mat (but strictly speaking that should be $1\frac{1}{3}$-oz mat).

22

Thus one could laminate a hull in one layer of Fabmat. This is difficult for the amateur because it is slow to wet out and requires special techniques to do so. In addition the off-cuts are expensive waste.

Resin

Manufacturers use various descriptions for their resins. There are around 200 different resins for different purposes. The prefix will describe its purpose, the number describes its type, and the suffix tells whether it is pre-accelerated or not. For example AP 101 PA means 'All-purpose, type 101, pre-accelerated'. GC 150 PA means 'Gelcoat, type 150, pre-accelerated'. There will also be a batch number on the drum. The basic manufacturer will give full details on his drum, which is usually 500 lb size, or sometimes 55 lb (25 kilo). The secondary supplier, the firm which specialises in supplying canoeing people, will often decant from 500 lb drums into their own smaller drums or cans and stick on their own labels, which do not give the batch numbers, only the type number.

All polyester resins are made in the same way and work in the same way. Some resins are thin and runny, like water, and some are thick and stiff, like a paste. But they are all polyester resin.

Laminating resin is thin and runny, so as to penetrate the binder on the mat or the fibres of the cloth. It will drain out of any glass mat or cloth with which it is laid up unless it sets hard within a fairly short time, say two or three hours. Laminating resin cannot be used for the gelcoat, as it drains off the vertical areas of the moulds.

Gelcoat resin is made with a thickening additive, which makes it thixotropic: literally, it will stay where it is put. This resin is used for the surface coat of the boat, and is laid into the moulds without glass reinforcement. The ideal thickness for gelcoat is 20 thousands of an inch, about $\frac{1}{50}$". Quite often this resin is used for putting patches on to the boat as it keeps the patch in place because of its thixotropic qualities.

Warm conditions cause the resins to become runnier when wet and to set more quickly when catalysed. If resins are stored in cool conditions, as they should be, then take care that the resins are put into the workshop to attain room temperatures overnight before use. Cold gelcoat, about 10°C, is too stiff to apply easily.

The curing time varies from resin to resin, but in general for novice work a slowish-curing resin, with a long pot life is needed. If the resin is a fast-setting type, then a novice builder should mix small quantities. A long pot life is forty-five minutes at 65°F, and a fast-setting type has a fifteen-minute pot life at 65°F. A large mix is 6 lb, and a small mix is about $1\frac{1}{2}$ to 2 lb. Gelcoat will set in about ten minutes with a normal mix at 65°-70°F (18°-20°C). Laminating resin sets more slowly, usually in about forty-five minutes.

A long green life gives one more latitude when trimming casts. A short green life indicates an early cure, but leaves less time for trimming. When resin begins to set, during its green stage, it generates heat, and the end blocks of a canoe can get so hot as to discolour the canoe shell. Fire dangers do exist. If resin in the pot goes off quickly and the jelly-like lump is dropped into the waste bin, be careful because the considerable heat that it may generate could start a fire.

Resin is not particularly inflammable, and a cast job requires a lot of heating, but once it gets going there is a fierce black-smoked fire, rather like that when rubber tyres burn, and difficult to extinguish. Green resin in a pot, may be a hot mix, that is one which is going off very quickly, can develop so much exotherm that it begins to smoke and to crackle. This is a dangerous condition, and it should be put out in a clear area to cool off. There is a characteristic stench, and the slight crackling noise is noticeable.

Resin will keep at normal room temperatures for about 2 years, but in summertime gelcoat has been known to 'go off' in 3 months. Do not store resin in a store room which is heated by central heating pipes.

Glass/resin ratio
The usual proportion of glass mat to resin is 2 parts of glass to 5 parts of resin by weight. If one uses woven materials the proportion of glass in the final laminate is increased. A resin-rich job, which is typical of novice work, is not a bad fault, but it

24

does add weight without much increasing the strength. A resin-dry job is poor because the laminate cannot develop its potential strength and stiffness, and it will be porous.

Chapter 2

The workshop

Layout
This drawing represents a basically good system.

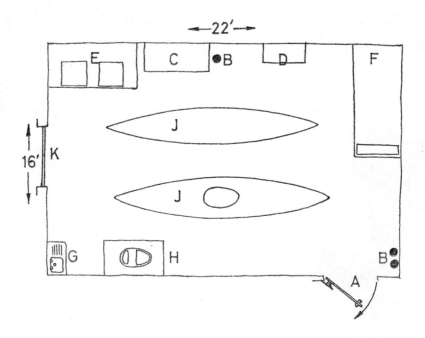

Workshop layout

A   A door, opening outwards, with a spring closure. This is a basic fire precaution.

B   Several fire extinguishers, placed handy to the likely seat of the fire, and to the door out of which one first rushes in panic, and then through which one returns to put out the fire.

C   The resin and cleaner store, a large lockable bin, in this case made of steel, galvanised, 6 ft by 3 ft by 2 ft, with a lockable lid.

D   A metal office cupboard, with steel shelves, lockable, in which the pigments and odds and ends, tools etc are kept.

E   The resin mixing bench.

F   The glass table and rolls of glass.

G   A sink with cold water on tap and an electric water heater. Gas has a dangerous naked flame for a pilot light.

H   The details bench where the cockpits are made.

J   The deck and hull moulds on their trestles.

K   A window for ventilation and possible fire escape. One must compromise between containing the warmth of the workshop on a cold day, and letting out warm air with the fumes, so slowing down the job. A long session in a fume-laden atmosphere has the same effect on the average adult male as a fair bit of drink, and it is not noticeable until into the fresh air you go, and set off to drive home.

Occasionally after I have had a twelve-hour stretch of concentrated work, my wife tells me she can smell the stench of resin on my breath, even after a good hot bath or shower, which seems to indicate that the body absorbs the fumes in some way. The effect on children would be bad if they were in either a *heavily* contaminated atmosphere for an hour or two, or a less heavily contaminated atmosphere all day. The effects depend on the concentration of fumes and time exposed to them. Be careful when using acetone or brush cleaner.

Since I used this room, six years have passed, and my present workshop is 36 ft by 24 ft and 12 ft high, with three working bays and twelve sets of moulds stacked ready for use. This is rather advanced for the average small group building a few canoes each winter, so I have referred to the smaller earlier set-up in which good working systems developed.

Resin mixing equipment
A metal tray (A) which can be burned off is useful, or a piece of old hardboard which can be thrown away when fouled up with resin drips will do.

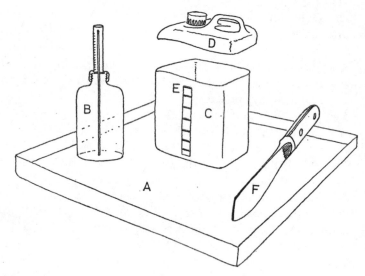

Resin-mixing equipment

B is a plastic measuring bottle for liquid catalyst. The bottle is squeezed and the liquid rises in the inner tube and spills over into the outer measuring tube. When the required amount is in the outer tube the catalyst is poured into the resin.

C is a typical plastic 1-gallon jar, usually obtainable from soft drink manufacturers and so on, as syrups, detergents, and all kinds of household liquids are sold in them. Ensure that the interior is clean before use. Wash out the bottle with water, then with a little brush cleaner sloshed around inside with the top on, and then cut around the bottle just below the top. Keep the top piece (D) as a handy tray for odd jobs, like the gelcoat for the seat, or filler for some odd job.

It is recommended to measure resin by weight, but a spring balance can frequently become gummed up with spilled resin, and does not receive the care it should have. As a general rule the resin weighs one pound per inch of these pots. If you want to check this, weigh out a pound of resin into one of these jars, having first stuck a strip of masking tape up the side. Mark this level on the paper. You should find it is about one inch from the bottom of the jar. Carry on filling up the jar, marking off the level at one pound intervals (E). Soon you will find that you can estimate the weight of resin within an ounce or so on sight.

F is a putty knife, or palette knife, and is used for spooning out colour pastes and for stirring the resin. An old table knife is almost as good, as is a wooden stick which has the advantage of being disposable.

Laminating equipment

The items illustrated are what I use, but a simple 2″ brush will do. A is a quite cheap soft woollen-surfaced roller from Woolworths, called 'Handirolla'. It is 5″ long, and about $2\frac{1}{2}$″ in diameter. It works by putting down resin on dry areas of glass, and picks up resin from resin rich areas, thus making the best use of resin and avoiding soggy patches. The trade use mohair rollers, which are quite expensive but do a better job. I find

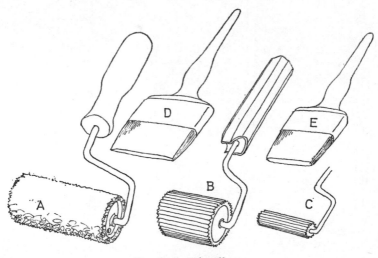

Brushes and rollers

novices all too ready to ruin rollers by forgetting about them until they have gone hard.

B is a hard-ribbed roller, 2″ in diameter and 2″ long. It has a plastic handle, is easy to keep clean and does a splendid job. The smaller diameter roller, C, is used for cockpit rim rolling where the ability to follow a tight curvature is needed.

D is a 3″ brush which I find better for putting on gelcoat, but only after the brush has been used once for laminating, thus shedding its surplus fibres in the laminate where it doesn't matter.

E is a 2″ brush which is generally useful and basic equipment.

The glass table
It is not essential to have a glass table for one-off jobs, but that

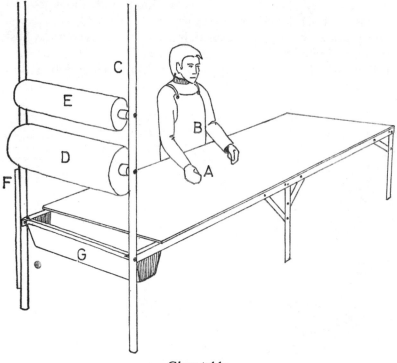

Glass table

illustrated is fairly standard practice in any grp workshop. For one-off jobs, cutting on the kitchen lino is quite sufficient, but hide the cuts under the rug.

A is the cutting top, a piece of hardboard 4 ft by 8 ft. Best of all is a sheet of plate glass, but this is expensive. The worker (B) usually stands, if he is right-handed, so that the rolls of glass are on his right. In our workshop the rolls of glass are suspended on two upright parallel alloy tubes (C), socketed into the concrete floor, and bolted to the roof supports. D is a roll of glass mat, which is free to rotate on a cross tube of alloy. So long as the cross-tube is near enough exactly long enough to fill the space between the uprights, one bolt should be fixed to the upright by its nut and enter the tube about one inch. The bolt at the other end is not fixed in any way, simply being pushed into the upright and so into the open tube. It too should enter about one inch.

E is a roll of woven rovings, and we always have some handy now as it is so useful for building semi-lightweight canoe hulls.

F is a straight edge of alloy, $1\frac{1}{2}''$ by $\frac{1}{8}''$, about 40" long. G is a tray for scraps.

Trestles and slings
Instead of trestles, the kitchen table will do, but a regular workshop will find the need for plenty of trestles. We have three working bays, and use two trestles per bay, and then there are often not enough, with some moulds being worked on and others waiting for resin to set.

The trestles (A) are made from slotted angle, from seven pieces each 4 ft long and several small bracing pieces. This puts the cross-braced ends about 4 ft apart, which is quite far enough. Wider than that and the mould flanges will catch on the cross bar which is a nuisance when working single-handed. The upper ends of the crossed ends should be well padded to avoid scratching new canoes and plugs.

B is the worker, complete with apron and old shoes. He is there to show at what height the canoe moulds or the finished shell should be slung—when the cockpit is being fitted, for example. The slings (C) are strong nylon cord which run over alloy tube fixed up in the roof space. These loops should be

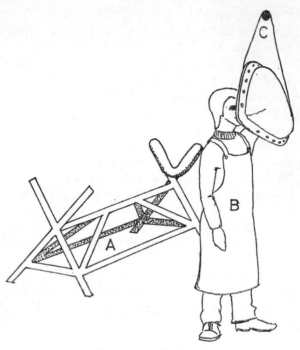

Trestles and slings

about 4 ft apart. If you sling the canoe too close to the ends, the cord will slip off the end of the canoe; on one occasion this dropped on to the end of a saw-horse, kicking into the air a pot of resin which then goo-ed up everything for yards around.

Jointing equipment
A is a saw-horse (useful for many other purposes), which has on it a sheet of alloy (B), about 2 ft by 8″, which is used as a wetting-out board. A piece of cardboard will do for this for one-off jobs. C is the resin pot, and D a 2″ wetting-out brush.

E is the central horizontal pole of an older-type TV aerial, but a piece of wood will do. It should be long enough to reach the end of the canoe from the cockpit hole. About 5 ft long is right. If wood is stiff enough it is too heavy to handle easily, and if it is light enough it is not stiff enough to guide the brush properly. The end of the pole should be flattened as shown in

32

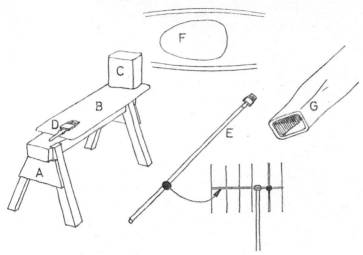

Set-up for joining

G so that the brush slots in without shaving to fit. This is suitable for poles of about $\frac{3}{4}''$ diameter. Wider poles should be flattened to an ellipse, into which the brush is jammed up to its shoulders. A slack brush will fall out up the far end of the canoe.

F is the canoe mould set on edge at about waist height. It is easy to do this with a trestle as illustrated, but without that one can wedge the moulds upright by using four chairs, two at each end, opposed to each other so that the backs hold the mould on edge. Do cover any tapestry upholstery with some protective material.

Some workshop tools
In a workshop that has been running for some years, one finds many different tools for different purposes. Those illustrated are the most useful.

A   The basic trimming knife. Indispensable.
B   The padsaw blade in the same handle.
C   The standard coping saw which, being slight, can break easily.
D   A standard frame bent to accommodate the Junior hacksaw blade.

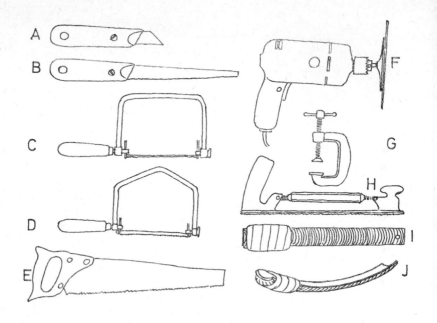

Some workshop tools

E   An ordinary handsaw, used for cutting all kinds of grp
    materials. The more modern multi-purpose saw with speci-
    ally hardened blade would be preferable.
F   A two-speed electric drill and sanding disc.
G   A junior 'G' clamp, 3". The usual woodwork clamps are
    too big.
H   A special bodywork tool which takes blades as illustrated
    at 'I'. It can be curved by using the bottlescrew adjuster.
I   The milled body file with coarse cut teeth. It is useful to
    use it without a handle, but with the end wrapped in tape,
    so that the hand is not lacerated by the sharp teeth.
J   A rare tool. It is a curved half-round milled file, and its
    uses in making plugs are many, as it cuts hollow curves
    with great accuracy.
    In addition there is a metalworker's vice and a woodworker's
vice, a hacksaw, a brace and socket wrench for trapped nut
moulds, a drawer full of drill bits, coping saw blades and cutting blades, plus fittings for the drill, a jig saw and an orbital

sander. The cost of all this is considerable but one can get by on much less, specifically a trimming knife, a coping saw, a hand drill and one or two bits, and a screwdriver.

Scrap aluminium

Your local scrapyard is a friendly place. They are really helpful. Look in the yellow pages for a 'Scrap Merchant. Non-ferrous metals'. Go and find him. It is probably somewhere in the old part of a town, or in a new industrial estate. Ask the yard manager, who is usually found by the weighbridge, for help. What you want are:

1 Alloy poles, 2" diameter, such as are used for TV aerials. Take them complete with clamps, but take off the clamps before they are weighed, or you will pay alloy price for light scrap, and it is not worth it. Ask for the clamps to be 'thrown in' afterwards.
2 Alloy sheet. Usually van panels, sides from wrecked lorries. Some quite big pieces of new material can also be found.
3 TV aerial rods, about 1" diameter and about 5 ft long.

Wear old clothes because you will have to scramble about on a tottering heap of junk, and vast heaps of old rags and papers will be nearby. A van is better for taking away the materials. Cars tend to collect dirt. A canoe roof-rack carries the poles very well.

These materials are used as follows.

1 2" poles. Lengths from 4 ft to 12 ft. Racking canoes and moulds, and making workshop racking for glass rolls, a useful glass table frame, even trailer parts and slalom gates.
2 Sheet. Wetting-out boards, 'shuttering' for making grp panels, details such as the foot-brace bracket, 'fences' and slips for rigging up plugs, and for correcting gross fractures in canoes.
3 1" by 5 ft poles. These are ideal for brush extension rods when making deck-hull joints.

Racks and stands in alloy tube

LUGLESS JOINTS. The idea is to make a racking system for a workshop, or even a display stand for an exhibition, using the materials to hand. Alloy lugs and clamps are expensive, but the tubes may be 'welded' together using glass and resin, as follows.

Chalk out the framework on to the workshop floor, breaking it down into flat panels which can be erected and joined up later. Joints which are to be permanent are treated differently from those to be removable. Calculate the number of removable joints needed.

Each joint needs a 4" collar, so 6 joints need 24" of collar material. Clean and polish and coat with release agent a 2-ft length of the tubing to be used. The diameter must be correct for the eventual joint. Cut enough glass cloth, or woven rovings, to go twice around the pole for a length of 2 ft. Mix a small quantity of gelcoat, and coat the prepared pole with this, wrap on the cloth, and continue coating with gelcoat. Make neat and tidy close to the pole, and leave it to set. (Mat goes baggy and makes a poor lumpy collar, and laminating resin is so wet that it drips all over the place, and the cloth unwinds before it can set.) When 'green', slit lengthways, and leave to set hard. When it is hard, after say a day, peel the cloth off the pole, and cut it into the necessary lengths for the sockets.

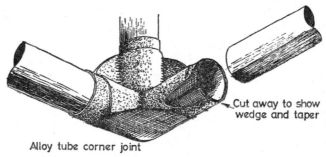

Cut away to show wedge and taper

Alloy tube corner joint

G r p joints for alloy tubes

For every joint needed, make a joining plate of 3-oz laminate in mat on an alloy plate or sheet, polished, with no gelcoat, the finished plate being about 5" square. However, if a horizontal frame is to turn up into a vertical frame, at the turn-up points the alloy wetting-out sheet or plate can be bent to the angle required, and the laminate made on the curved plate. The curve should be made around a piece of the pole.

Having made all the necessary grp plates, assemble the cut

lengths of cleaned up alloy pole on the chalk marks. Brace them into position with anything heavy to stop them rolling about. Place a joining plate under the joint at each crossing place. It will be necessary to cut one tube where it crosses the other, so that both lie in the same plane. However, it is possible for uncut poles to cross each other, in which case the lower pole is laid in place, the joining plate over it, then the upper pole is laid across, thus trapping the plate at the joint.

PERMANENT JOINTS. Prepare resin and some $1\frac{1}{2}$-oz glass mat pieces. Pre-wet the glass and drape it across the poles to be joined. When it is wetted out, form it into place with a brush, easing it well under the curve of the pole. Two or even three layers of mat are right. Leave to set hard. In the case of crossing poles, it is now necessary to turn the frame over and to make the joint to the joint plate on the other side also.

SOCKET JOINT. Wax the end of the pole to be joined. Slip a slit collar over it. Use tiny chips of resin to keep the edges of the slit slightly apart to ease the joint the right amount. Sometimes it is useful only to ease the open end of the socket in this way, then the pole enters into a very slight taper, and usually when it is finished the joint is a dead snug fit.

With the socket lined up exactly on the end of the pole, lay it in place, block it into position, with the slit downwards against the joining plate. Glass over the collar as for the simpler permanent joint. When it is hard, twist the pole out, and the joint is made.

After this work, the joints will be raggy and messy-looking. Trim them clean with a coping saw, and sand them off with a disc sander. Paint all over with coloured resin, using masking tape on the polished alloy poles, which leaves a neat line when removed, provided the resin is still wet.

A stand made to support an eskimo kayak at the Crystal Palace Canoeing Exhibition in February 1972 had an 'H'-form floor frame, with an upright pole at one end of the cross-bar of the 'H' which carried a table, and a socket formed around the end of an eskimo kayak, at the other end of the cross-bar, which supported an eskimo kayak vertically in balance. Joints in the racking in the roof of the workshop, tubes end to end, were made using the socket system (described above) *in situ*.

37

Canoe Building

First-aid cabinet

There are many small cuts and scratches and irritations from spikes or splinters of glass which stick in the skin like rose thorns. Very rarely one may have a splash of catalyst in the eye. Quite often a skin irritation like a slight nettle rash will develop on young tender skin, but this usually subsides after a few hours after a good wash in hot water.

The first aid cabinet should contain the following:

1 2% solution of sodium bicarbonate
2 Eye bath
3 Tweezers
4 Sterile needles
5 Sticky plasters for small cuts
6 Scissors for cutting plaster strip
7 Sterile swabs in packets
8 Two or three wound dressings.

Catalyst attacks human flesh, causing deep persistent burns. It is soluble in water, so any splashes on the skin, especially around the face and eyes, must be washed off with copious quantities of water at once. Delay of more than a few seconds results in intense pain.

In the rare event of catalyst splashes in the eye, immediately turn the cold tap full on and using the hands as a scoop, cause the rush of water to flow into the eyes whilst blinking rapidly. It is not easy, and water rushes up the nose too, but it is better than losing the sight of an eye. About two minutes of being half-drowned will clear the eye of any catalyst traces, and that is usually enough. However, in the case of irritation remaining, bathe the eye with the sodium bicarbonate solution. Do not use any ointment on the eye.

Fire precautions

Resins and solvents present a fire risk. Resin does not easily ignite, but acetone solvents do. When a fire blazes up it does so fiercely; one jumps back away from it in alarm, and later one thinks of tackling it. Solvents float on water. Water will spread flaming solvents to other parts of the workshop. A puddle of water from a leaking roof will hold spilled solvent as a thin skin and spread it widely, behind shelves, around drums, under

38

tables. When it catches the flames run everywhere that the water has taken the solvent. Pockets of gas from evaporated solvent will form up in the roof, and when these flash they do so as a minor explosion, taking flame and smoke many yards away from the seat of the fire, shattering glass in skylights, baring electric cables, and stripping paint from walls and ceilings.

Bearing this in mind,

1 Keep solvents and resins in bulk in drums inside a lockable metal bin.

2 Keep loose cans of colour pastes, catalyst dispenser etc in a lockable steel cupboard. An old filing cabinet is suitable.

3 Place the resins and solvents as far from the doors as is reasonable and against an outside wall if possible.

4 Never have a naked light, even a pilot light in a gas geyser, in the workshop.

5 The fire risk should be concentrated in one place so that as one jumps backwards away from the flare-up, there is a door behind one.

6 The fire extinguishers should be kept outside the doors, on a wall bracket at shoulder level, so that when the door is open the extinguisher is clearly seen, not hidden by the door.

7 The extinguishers should be powder or foam. Water types may put out flames on walls, and so on, but the wasted water will spread flaming solvents even further. The powder type, although expensive, is effective.

8 It is usual to have old clothes and overalls hanging inside the door on hooks. The clothes become stained and soaked with resin drips. This is a source of fire just within the door, and should not be there. It is preferable to have the working overalls hanging outside the resin workshop.

9 A large notice fixed to the door concerning the hazards of working with synthetic resins can be a safeguard for the responsible person from the insurance point of view.

10 It is better also to have large 'No Smoking' notices fixed all around the walls of the workshop.

11 In one case a fire was caused because a boy lit a cigarette, successfully closed his lighter, and tried to put it in his

pocket. He missed his pocket, the lighter trigger struck the ground, and the lighter sparked and fired the solvent skin on a puddle of water. It may be enough danger simply to have a lighter and, say, a handkerchief in the same pocket in the workshop.

12   If one is responsible for a group of children who are working on the canoe, it is potentially dangerous to leave them for as little as five minutes, as they will light cigarettes, and dodging 'Sir' and authority is part of the game for many.

Chapter 3

Building a grp canoe

Working speed

All novices will start tentatively, and there is little one can do but nag them into quicker work. In general, the faster one works the better the job will be. The more skilful one becomes

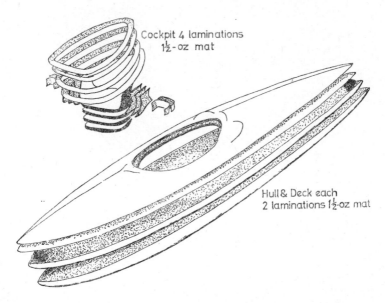

Cockpit 4 laminations
1½-oz mat

Hull & Deck each
2 laminations 1½-oz mat

Cutting pattern for heavy canoe

the faster one is working. Until confidence in accuracy is gained you will not find that effortless speed in laminating. If you are not quick, then resin setting problems are found, which the expert is able to deal with, but hardly ever comes across in his fast workmanship. The aim is 'a sense of urgency without haste'.

BUILDING SEQUENCE

1 Workshop clean and ready
2 Materials all to hand
3 Brushes clean and ready
4 Mixing pots clean and ready
5 Sharp blades in trim knives
6 Part-used brush for gelcoat ready
7 Barrier cream on hands and forearms
8 Polish moulds
9 Cut glass
10 Apply release agent to moulds for deck, hull and cockpit
11 Make stiffener former
12 Apply gelcoat to moulds
13 Make footrest flanges
14 Clean brushes
15 Make buoyancy blocks
16 Trim stiffener former
17 Check that deck gelcoat is ready for laminating
18 Mix 4 lbs of lay-up resin for deck
19 Laminate mat on to deck mould
20 Mix 2 lbs of lay-up resin for deck
21 Laminate extra mat thickness over foredeck
22 Laminate cloth around cockpit area
23 Check lamination and trimming edges on deck
24 Clean soft roller, hard roller and brushes
25 Clean hands with brush cleaner
26 Shape footrest flanges and drill bolt holes
27 Attach flanges to footrest-placing jig
28 Check that hull gelcoat is ready for laminating
29 Mix 5 lbs of lay-up resin for hull
30 Laminate mat into hull
31 Place extra thicknesses at bow and stern

32 Mix 2-3 lbs of lay-up resin for hull
33 Laminate cloth into hull
34 Place stiffener former in position
35 Mix 1-2 lbs lay-up resin for hull
36 Laminate over stiffener former
37 Double-thickness stiffener in the centre two feet of hull
38 Fit footrest flanges
39 Trim deck and cockpit hole
40 Check lamination and trimming edges on hull
41 Clean soft roller finally, and put away
42 Clean hard rollers and brushes
43 Clean hands with brush cleaner
44 Trim deck and cockpit hole
45 Check that cockpit gelcoat is ready for laminating
46 Laminate cockpit
47 Check lamination and trimming edges on cockpit
48 Clean brushes and hands
49 Trim hull
50 Release footrest jig
51 Bolt hull to deck
52 Set out wetting-out board
53 Mix 1 lb of lay-up resin for joint
54 Make joint
55 Mix 2 oz of laminating resin/glass scraps dough for end blocks
56 Place end blocks
57 Clean brushes
58 Clean extension pole
59 Clean hands
60 Trim cockpit
61 Make footrest bar
62 Check that joining strip has set
63 Remove moulds from deck-hull
64 Clean mould flanges of resin flakes
65 Wash out moulds with soft wet sponge
66 Put moulds away
67 Place hull-deck on trestles
68 Trim flash with file
69 Fit buoyancy blocks

43

70   Clean brush
71   Release cockpit from mould
72   Clean up cockpit cast
73   Sling deck-hull, clamp in cockpit
74   Fit cockpit
75   Clean brush and hands
76   Drill end holes
77   Trim cockpit-deck joint
78   Put canoe on trestles
79   Fit seat braces
80   Apply trim-line masking tape, both sides
81   Mix 2 oz of gelcoat for right-side trim line
82   Apply right-side trim line
83   Remove masking tape on right-side trim line
84   Mix 2 oz of gelcoat for left-side trim line
85   Apply left-side trim line
86   Remove masking tape on left-hand trim line
87   Clean brush and hands
88   Sweep floor, tidy up rubbish, tidy benches
89   Put rubbish bin outside
90   Check that trim lines are hard enough not to smear
91   Fit end loops
92   Some finishing touches
93   Clean and put away all equipment
94   Clean hands thoroughly
95   Cleanser cream on hands
96   Good wash in hot water and soap
97   Record details
98   Use it
99   Knock it about a bit
100   Enjoy it

1   Workshop clean and ready
It is quite possible to work in a workshop that is deep in rubbish, which has drifts of bits in corners and tools and pots which are festooned in glass and resin bits. Even the best of workshops tends to look rather like this after a hard day turning out only one boat.

However, one learns to avoid this state of affairs in course of time. The messy stage is reached and recognised and passed by; after a few dozen canoes, one learns to work cleanly, and the workshop reflects this ability, unconsciously to work well.

You may not achieve this effortless cleanliness first time, but do try. Begin with clean surroundings and tools.

Pay especial attention to these items.

a   Floor. Is it clean and tidy?
b   Rubbish bin. Is it empty?
c   Glass table. Is it clear and clean, and is the glass roll on its rack?
d   Brushes. Are all the handles clean, the bristles flexible and clean?
e   Extension handle. Is it completely free of all hairy bits of glass?
f   The rollers. Do they turn easily? Are the ribs clear of resin?
g   Mixing pots. Are all contaminants washed out, and used pots flaked clean?
h   Are the warning notices in place and visible?
i   Is adequate ventilation assured?
j   Is the place warm enough?

2   Materials all to hand
Having studied this section you should know what materials you will need. Have the gelcoat resin there, the laminating resin, glass, barrier cream, cleaner and so on. It happened once that the catalyst had been locked in a safe place for fire precautions, and when everyone assembled to start work, it was found that the key was with the man in charge who happened to be away that day.

3   Brushes clean and ready
A brush which is solid with resin and one which is soft and ready for use look much the same a short way off. Pick them up, flex them in the fingers, be satisfied that they will do what is required. If they are not soft enough or clean enough, then clean them again.

45

4 Mixing pots clean and ready

The slightest colour contamination in a mixing pot can foul up a whole boat, especially in the gelcoat which is the first resin that is applied. Flakes of hard colourless resin will also transfer to the job and refuse to lay down, and so produce delamination blisters in the final boat. A pot with the slightest trace of chemical which may affect the resin will inhibit setting rates for hours, even days, and it may be almost unnoticeable so slight is the amount present. Ensure that each new pot is cleaned out with brush cleaner before using it.

5 Sharp blades in trim knives

A trim knife blade will last for several canoes. Toward the end of its useful life it will cease to cut glass cleanly and will start to drag the fibres, making a raggy cut. Also, when trimming the waste edge away it is difficult to get a clean cut, and this leads to a raggy-looking joint line.

It is an economy each time to fit a new blade into the knife handle. It is possible to sharpen knives, but the tip of the blade, which is a neat angular point, tends to become rounded and again a tidy cut is prevented, even with a sharp blade. Spend a few pence, therefore, and buy a new blade for each boat. The attitude of mind this reflects is that of the mind that *will* produce a good, well-built canoe.

6 Part used brush for gelcoat ready

It should be possible, with forethought, to have a partly-used brush ready for use to apply the gelcoat. One which has been used once only for laminating is ideal, since most laminating brushes are inclined to shed their bristles (use brushes with white bristles rather than black as they do not show so clearly in a laminate if they come out). The once-used brush has probably shed its quota of loose bristles into the lamination of the previous boat, so is less likely to leave spare bristles in the gelcoat, which does tend to show on the surface of the boat.

It is sometimes useful, if this is the first boat ever, to wash the new brush out very firmly in a pot of clean brush cleaner, manipulating it with the fingers and swishing it about in the fluid for several minutes. Incidentally, if you are using a cheap brush which is not specifically for grp work, you will probably find that the handle is painted with a pretty coloured and glossy paint. This is almost always soluble in brush cleaner, so the handle first becomes sticky then starts to shed its quota of colour into the job or the brush cleaner. If this is the case, strip the handle of colour first or it will cause problems later in the work.

7 *Barrier cream on hands and forearms*
Now is the time to apply barrier cream to hands and forearms, especially nail beds and wrists.

8 *Polish moulds*
Use a good wax for this, perhaps Mirrorglaze or Formula C. Simoniz or Slipwax are about as good and less expensive. A cheap wax, carnauba, is available, and does as well from the separation aspect, but a high-quality finish is much harder to achieve with the cheaper wax. A silicone wax must *not* be used. See glossary notes.

When polishing, always by hand, ensure that the mould is clear of all flakes of resin. Previous casts may have had a bleed-through of resin from a joint, and this penetrates the gap which sometimes exists between the cast and the mould surface. The bleed-through then hardens as a flake on to the mould, and being clear is usually difficult to see. A quick brushing over with the finger tips, especially around the mould edges, will reveal these flakes. They should be gently eased off the mould surface.

Polish the mould surface by hand, rubbing on the wax with a wax-soaked cloth. Use small rotating movements, plus long sweeps first lengthways and then crossways on the mould. If you can cover the whole surface quickly, in about 10-15 minutes, then you can do the whole job at one go. Otherwise you should stop half-way and do it in two sections. I take areas about 2 ft long and half the mould-width across, and apply the polish area by area along the whole mould.

If a machine and polishing mop is used there can be severe local overheating, and tiny air bubbles expand under the surface; these burst through, and spoil the mould. Work by hand.

Using a clean cloth (the type of material used for cotton vests is ideal), the wax surface is cut back, and a dull polish begins to show. Do not persevere with this cloth, as it quickly picks up surplus wax which is re-applied and so waxy smears appear. Keep turning the cloth so that a clean wax-free surface is applied to the unpolished wax. Do the whole mould from end to end.

Follow up with another perfectly clean, wax-free cloth, and give it the final polishing. It may be necessary to work at some streaks of wax here and there, left over by the first polishing.

Certain points to remember in polishing a mould have appeared in my experience as follows.

a   Apply polish to the mould flanges. There is no need to shine these. If this is not done the flanges could be stuck together by the resin bleed-through on joining.

b   Polish the smooth, shiny side of the mould, not the fibrous outer surface. Not one but several groups of quite intelligent people have indeed 'polished the moulds' all over!

c   *DO NOT USE MOULD CLEANER* Mirrorglaze is produced as a wax polish, *and* as a mould glaze and cleaner which removes wax. If you use the cleaner, not the wax, the mould will be beautiful, and glitter like a star, but when the cast is made it will become as one with the mould, and so there will be a useless £85 worth of mould, and a useless £15 worth of canoe, irretrievably sealed together.

d   Wax build-up occurs if too much wax is applied to the moulds. This is when the surface of the mould takes on a gritty appearance, like a fine sand, dulled, rather like ground glass. The wax has been applied and has hardened in this gritty way, and it cannot be removed by polishing with soft cloths. It is necessary to cut down the whole mould surface with machine cleaner or mould glaze and cleaner and a polishing mop in a drill, and then thoroughly to repolish the moulds. This problem is usually found with moulds which have been much used. Wax build-up leaves tell-tale dull patches on the finished canoe.

9   Cut glass

There are a number of different ways in which material can be cut to make canoes. The basic and simplest way is to make everything of two layers of chopped strand mat, $1\frac{1}{2}$ oz specific weight. The cockpit seat and rim will be twice that. Such a lay-up will produce a solo slalom canoe of about 35-40 lbs weight. However, it is possible to lighten the canoe without seriously weakening it. The various options are discussed on pages 98-101, mostly in relation to the Streamlyte KW 7 slalom kayak which moulds are available for sale from the makers.

'Standard 3-oz lay-up' describes the weight of glass that goes into a square foot of the finished job. It can be made of two layers of $1\frac{1}{2}$-oz mat, or three layers of 1-oz mat, or some other combination, for example one layer of 2-oz mat and one layer of 9-oz cloth (remember cloth is weighed per square yard). However, the average amateur builder will either have cut lengths of material from a kit for a one-off job, or he will have perhaps one roll of mat, enough for six canoes probably. He will not have enough resources to buy a roll of cloth, which is more than double what a roll of mat will cost; nor will he have the resources to buy two or three rolls of mat of different specific weights. He may have bought a tea chest of scrap material from some works using the material, and this may contain a variety of scraps, but when you work out the cost per square foot of the scrap material you use, compared with what you must throw away, the cost is so near to that of new first-class material that you may as well buy new, and save some headaches.

The drawing (page 41) shows the cutting pattern for a 3-oz boat using only $1\frac{1}{2}$-oz mat, and this is probably the favourite lay-up of the novice canoe builder. The boat is heavy, durable, and strong if properly made. It requires the minimum resources in terms of rolls of this and that, and is recommended for this reason. However, it does cut across my basic qualities in a canoe which are, remember:

a   It must look good
b   It must be light to carry—40 lbs is too much for a thirteen year old
c   It must handle well.

There are many ways in which to cut the glass for a canoe or kayak, but this method turns out semi-lightweight canoes of around 30 lbs, plus or minus 2 lbs. The drawing shows the pattern to use.

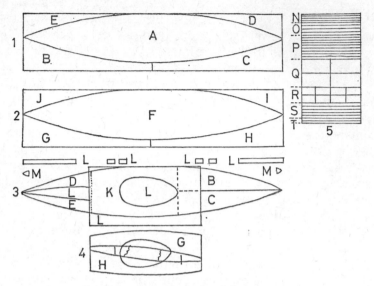

Cutting pattern for solo slalom kayak

1   A piece of 1½-oz chopped strand mat, the length of the boat and 3 ft wide. A is the piece necessary for the hull of the boat. The off-cuts B and C make the bow deck portions. Parts D and E make up part of the rear deck.

2   This is a piece of 10-oz woven rovings, the length of the boat and 3 ft wide. F is the piece necessary for the hull for the second lamination. Parts G and H are used later on the deck to reinforce the area around the cockpit (see section 4). Parts I and J help to fill in the small gaps between the edges of G and H.

3   K is a piece of 1½-oz chopped strand mat. It covers the area of the rear deck from where the pieces D, E and L end, allowing a 1″ overlap. This reaches up the foredeck to about 18″ in front of the cockpit, thus giving a double thickness just in front of the cockpit where it overlaps, with B and C. The central piece L and the edge piece L are used to make the hull bow and

50

stern thickening pieces and the seat braces. The end pieces M
are the end blocks made up from resin and glass mat scraps.
4 This shows the arrangement of pieces of woven rovings
around the cockpit.
5 This section of $1\frac{1}{2}$-oz mat is 3 ft wide and about 6 ft long.
N is four strips which make the keel stiffener. O is four wider
pieces by which the stiffener is laminated to the hull. The nine
pieces P are used for joining hull to deck, and the four pieces Q
are used for making the seat pan on the cockpit. R is eight
pieces which make up the two seat sides, and S is six pieces
which make the cockpit rim. T is two narrow pieces which are
used to stick the cockpit into the deck.

Using this method, the total length of glass mat used is 26 ft
of 3 ft wide material, and the cloth used is 14 ft by 3 ft. Resin
used is as follows:
Gelcoat: hull $1\frac{3}{4}$ lbs, deck $1\frac{1}{4}$ lbs, cockpit $\frac{1}{8}$ lb, total $3\frac{1}{8}$ lbs.
Laminating resin: hull 12 lbs, deck 8 lbs, cockpit 2 lbs, total
22 lbs. (This includes resin for joint.)

The total area of glass used is 78 sq ft of mat, which weighs
117 oz, or 7 lbs 5 oz. The cloth used is $4\frac{2}{3}$ sq yds, which at 10 oz
per square yard weighs 47 oz near enough, or 3 lbs almost.
Therefore the total weight of the canoe, including waste and
off-cuts, comes to 35 lbs 6 oz, call it $35\frac{1}{2}$ lbs. Allowing 3 lbs
waste, about 8% margin, the finished canoe should weigh about
$32\frac{1}{2}$ lbs. At present prices (November 1972) the way my workshop operates gives a price, per pound weight finished, of just
under 50p.

Ensure that the glass table surface is brushed clean, otherwise flakes and bits of rubbish can cause quite nasty delamination bubbles and colour blemishes.

The easiest way to cut glass is to cut around a hardboard pattern. First it is necessary to cut the pattern, and this is only
worthwhile if a large number of canoes is to be built, say 6 or
more. To cut the pattern it is first necessary to cut the glass on
the mould.

Cut a length of glass mat from the roll, the length of the
mould from bow to stern not including the flanges, plus one
inch. Lay the mat over the mould, hull first, and press it into
the mould so that one edge is about $\frac{1}{2}''$ one side of the mould

and the other waste edge is as wide as the mould requires. Few moulds ever require more than the width of the glass roll.

Using a very sharp trimming knife, and pressing down on to a slip of hardboard or alloy, trim around the mould edge, using the fingers to guide the knife blade so that a waste edge of about half an inch will stand up all round the mould when the job is laminated.

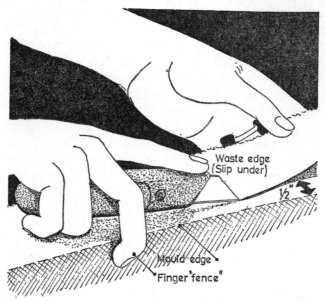

Cutting glass

Another method which can be used in order to cut glass accurately to the size required is to turn the mould upside down on the trestle with the hollow, shining surface underneath. The glass is laid over the outside of the mould and the cutting is done along the line of the angle between flange and mould. This is nearly enough the exact size required, and cutting with a trimming knife does not score the flange surface, at least not on the shining side.

Cut a slit in the bow end to identify it, then take the mat across to the table and, using it as a pattern, make a pattern or cut out the other layer of mat or woven rovings.

10 Apply release agent to moulds for deck, hull and cockpit
This is the PVA fluid, and is best applied by decanting a small amount, about a cupful, into a clean container. The fluid is spread on thinly by wiping it over the surface with a piece of soft sponge. On a newly-waxed surface the PVA may blob together, but a point will be found as the material dries out when the PVA is sticky enough to stay put and not to blob. It is very important to obtain an even spread of the release agent, with no uncovered places, otherwise the cast and the mould may be immovably fixed to each other. At best, small pieces of mould surface can be ripped out on separation.

11 Make stiffener former
Most slalom kayaks have rather flat bottoms, and this area is quite likely to bulge inward under normal water pressure. This puts a kink in the otherwise smooth bottom, spoiling the hydro-dynamics and eventually developing flexure cracks at the edges of the bulge. Earlier practice required thicker laminates, i.e. a 3-oz hull would be a minimum requirement. Now 2- or $2\frac{1}{2}$-oz hulls are normal and of course more flexible. To stop flexure, it is normal practice to build in a stiffener.

Recently the commercial firms have taken to laminating into the hull a long slip of wood, a simple 'D'-moulding as sold in woodwork shops, about $\frac{3}{4}''$ wide, $\frac{3}{8}''$ deep. For one-off jobs this may be the better choice, but instructions for a grp former follow.

A 12-ft length of alloy angle section, 1″ by 1″ and $\frac{1}{8}''$ thick is polished thoroughly on the inside of the angle and placed on blocks, with putty to hold it and the open side upwards. Laminate a single thickness of $1\frac{1}{2}$-oz mat along its length. Mix about a cupful of lay-up resin and lay four 3 ft by $1\frac{1}{4}''$ strips along the angle alloy. Paint it end to end with resin, pressed into the angle with the brush. Do this three times, until the former is well made, with no dry patches. When it is 'green', trim it neatly to the edge and leave it to harden ready for use.

12 Apply gelcoat to moulds
There is a technique in this which embodies the whole idea of grp work: 'urgency without haste'. The whole job should take

15 minutes, no more—two people working together can get on with it quickly, but single-handed working is described here.

Mix about 2 lbs of gelcoat for the average slalom hull. The mixing and colour choice is the same both for gelcoat and laminating resin. First one must choose what colour the boat is to be. 'Viking Orange' is a powerful deep orange colour which is seen well at a distance in poor visibility. Greys and greens and deep blues are not very clearly seen on the sea. Red, orange, yellow and perhaps white are good for visibility in full daylight. In the dusk, red appears black, and pale blue appears white. Under water, as when salvaging a sunken canoe, amber merges with Thames water and becomes almost invisible, but yellow is clearly seen.

On rivers the need for clearly visible boats is not so important, so some fancy alternatives are permissible, purple, black, blues, greens and so on.

The pigment is of two basic types, opaque and translucent. Also there is a metallic flake pigment which costs ten times what polychromatic pigment costs, so be cautious about what you order. It is possible to use household paint as a colouring agent but do not rely on the final colour being what you want. Children's poster powder paint can also be mixed in to some resin to give a colour, but you cannot be sure whether it is translucent or opaque.

When mixing, take a clean pot, measure out the required amount of resin into it, and then select the required colour. Spoon the colour paste into the resin with a palette knife. Gelcoat should be given a strong colour, the laminating resin should be less strongly coloured. Stir the colour into the resin very carefully, ensuring it is thoroughly distributed into every part of the resin. Gelcoat is a stiff resin, therefore difficult to mix easily. Add the catalyst in the correct proportion, about 5-7 mls per lb of resin. Stir carefully, taking care not to splash neat catalyst up into the eyes. The catalyst must be thoroughly distributed in the resin, otherwise partial curing faults will appear.

The proportion of catalyst to resin is variable. Some catalyst is double strength. On the whole, novices tend to work better with half-strength catalyst, as it is less sensitive to measuring errors. Follow the directions of the supplier when using catalyst. As a general rule the proportion is 2% by weight, catalyst to resin. Warm conditions, i.e. 65°F to 75°F will require less catalyst, conditions less warm, say 55°F to 65°F, require rather more catalyst in order to get the resin to 'go off' in a certain time. Cooler than 55°F finds setting times absurdly long, so the workshop temperature is important when estimating setting times. In general, the warmer the room, the less catalyst is required, but there should never be less than 2% by weight.

Take the pot in the left hand, the brush (free of loose bristles) in the right (if right-handed). Lay streaks of resin lengthwise on to the mould, the width of the brush and about a foot long, in a scooping motion, out of the pot straight on to the job in one easy flowing movement. If you find yourself using several strokes to put one streak on, you are wasting time—one sweep. Do *not* pour the resin into the mould and then spread it with the brush.

The streaks should be about 6″ apart, with one or two in the width at the bow, and say five or six in the centre. Work right from one end to the other in 3 or 4 minutes, no longer.

Go now, end to end, using the brush in firm across-the-mould sweeps at right-angles to the streaks. These brush strokes should be edge to edge, but it does not matter if you miss patches. Now sweep diagonally up to the edges from the centre line, end to end. Now with long sweeping strokes, moving right from the toes, using the whole body, flow the brush strokes from end to middle, lengthways. Skill in putting down the brush and lifting it off will give a smooth gelcoat, with little evidence of brush strokes. White is the most difficult colour of all to lay without evidence of streakiness on the finished canoe.

The gelcoat should be between 12 and 20 thousandths of an inch thick. It is impossible to measure it on to the job, but it can be checked afterwards by simple measurements with a micrometer. A good laminator will be laying down gelcoat within the required limits. The finished cast of the hull will be about $\frac{1}{16}$″, that of the deck about $\frac{3}{64}$″ thick. Extra thickening pieces will produce a shell thickness of about $\frac{1}{8}$″ at bow and stern keel line. The seat will be about $\frac{3}{16}$″ thick.

The temptation with novice builders, who almost invariably

are working slowly, is to persevere with resin as it begins to set. They do not wish to waste it. However, it begins to set in little pebbly nodules, which crumble into crumbs. Gelcoat will do this if the resin is not put on and spread quickly, i.e. in less than ten minutes. On the gelcoat, this causes the glass laminates which follow to be propped up away from the surrounding gelcoat. When the resin is hard, and out of the mould and in use, the ring-shaped air bubbles will break through leaving a little crater with a central pip. This is known as pebble-dash surface. If it happens with laminating resin, it will leave a rough surface on the laminate, and if this is where the knees go the knees will often be scrubbed painfully in that canoe. If the resin goes crumby, throw it away.

Wrinkled gelcoat can be caused by several things.

a Gelcoat too thin. Some people tend not to mix enough resin and so try to spread it out a long way, and it appears as a thin scrubby trace on the mould surface. It will often wrinkle, lacking strength to resist the laminating resin.

b Insufficient catalyst. This can be because not enough was put into the gelcoat or because the gelcoat which is thick was insufficiently stirred, and so some parts are catalysed, and some are not. The laminating resin will leach through and cause it to wrinkle.

c Heating the gelcoat locally to send it off. This can cause wrinkling because too much heat is generated in one spot.

One common and frustrating fault with many novice laminators is to mix up the resin, lay it in place, laminate beautifully into place all glass necessary, and then find that one has forgotten to put in catalyst. There are two main resins, the gelcoat and the laminating resin.

If the gelcoat is still wet on the hull, say, after 12 hours, then mix up about 100 cc of catalyst with about an equal quantity of brush cleaner, and paint this all over the wet gelcoat. This must be done as soon as possible, as the gelcoat starts to dry and becomes very sticky, thus resisting the penetration of the catalyst. Use the brush to stir up the gelcoat as much as possible and so disperse the catalyst/cleaner mixture as much as possible. This mixture is highly inflammable.

The cleaner leaches out and leaves the catalyst evenly distributed. Soon the surface of the gelcoat starts to harden. However, if the gelcoat is really thick, the catalyst may not penetrate completely, and the finished boat may be stuck in the mould by the wetness of the gelcoat in contact with the mould surface. It can be peeled out by persevering with plywood slips between cast and mould. After lamination, the thickness of the laminate may prevent penetration by the 'cocktail', but given time the resin will harden partially. One will have a soft boat, but it can be used.

13   Make footrest flanges

The footrest flange mould is already polished. No gelcoat is required, as it is not a surface job. Simply cut four pieces the size of the flange mould out of $1\frac{1}{2}$-oz mat. Prepare about $\frac{1}{4}$ lb of clear lay-up resin. Paint resin on to the mould. At once lay on one piece of glass. At once, without working the resin through, paint all over with more resin. Do the same with the second piece of mat. Lay on the third piece of mat, and paint again with resin. Lay on the fourth piece of mat, but do not paint with resin. Roll all over, as resin wets through. Roll about four times all over. If you have spare resin, paint this on too, and leave it. The whole job takes five minutes.

14   Clean brushes

The brush is the tool which requires the most frequent cleaning. Resin is held in the bristles, right up to the roots in the ferrule. It is easy to clean the lower ends of the bristles, but lack of care in cleaning up into the roots of the bristles causes a progressive build-up of hardened resin which quickly makes the brush useless, a sort of spatula with furry edges.

Resin when soaked out of the brush becomes suspended in the cleaner, and as it builds up into a thick sort of oily liquid, the suspended resin will set, much more slowly than on the boat, but it sets, and the pot of thickened cleaner becomes jelly-like and then hardens off. If one leaves a brush in this thick cleaner overnight, in the morning you will have a pot-sized slab of jelly with a convenient handle for lifting it out to throw into the bin.

The drawing shows the method we use; there are other ways,

but this suits us. Pot A contains cleaner which has collected a lot of bits and pieces, glass debris and flakes of hardened resin. It looks horrible, and we call it the gunge pot. Squash the brush down on to the bottom to press the resin in the brush out into the gunge. Then squeeze the bristles to expel the goo so that the drips fall back into the pot (B).

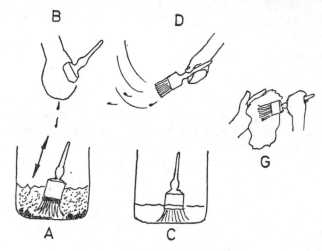

Cleaning the brushes

Next (C), use a little clean cleaner in which to leach out the remaining resin and goo from the brush. Slosh the brush about in this pot, then squeeze the cleaner out of it and flick the brush down on to the floor, or on to a suitable piece of cardboard placed to collect the drips. Flick clear of your trousers and the surroundings (D).

To finish off (G), take a *clean* piece of rag and soak a little clean cleaner on to it. Rub the brush on to this rag, so that the roots of the bristles are exposed to the clean rag.

In the course of work, the hands become sticky with setting resin, of varying colours. The handles of tools become encased in a mesh of glass strands and setting resin, a sort of cake gunge. It is good practice every half-hour or so quickly to clean the handles of all tools in use with cleaner, and wipe with a cleaner-damp cloth. It only takes one messy worker where four or five jobs are going on, and the spreading goo marks everything. Black is a particularly persistent colour, but it has been suggested that all novice builders should start with a white canoe, to learn quickly how important cleanliness is.

15   Make buoyancy blocks
Use polystyrene foam blocks, 2 ft by 3 ft, 4″ wide. From this raw material cut the blocks for each canoe. Each large block makes four quarter-size blocks, enough for two canoes. Each canoe therefore contains two blocks, one fore, one aft, each giving about 30 lbs buoyancy, total per canoe, 60 lbs. A waterlogged semi-lightweight canoe will float on its side in still water, half in and half out of the water, the waterline being about half-way up the centrally placed blocks.

If you have a pattern, it is simple. If you have not, then it must be a case of trial and error. Start with two blocks, each 12″ by 18″ by 4″. Using a felt-tipped marking pen, sketch in the curve of the deck ridge. The bow block is fitted about 2″ forward of the forward ends of the footrest flanges. The bow block tapers rather more than the stern block, which is fitted about 12″ to 14″ aft of the cockpit hole.

The lower edge of the block is cut to give a right-angled groove from end to end just large enough to fit over the stiffener rib. The top edge is cut to a slope to fit the deck slope. The toe is covered with masking tape; thin polythene sheet is permeable by resin, and it will attack the polystyrene even through polythene sheet.

16   Trim stiffener former
When the laminate is stiff enough to cut, slice along the edge of the alloy former with a sharp knife. Always cut away from the body, as the blade can snag; extra effort is put on to move the knife again, and it can come free with a rush and slip away to one side out of control. New blades go through human flesh like a hot knife through butter, but some young people with unscarred skins seem not to know about this simple precaution.

17   Check that deck gelcoat is ready for laminating
The way to check if gelcoat has set sufficiently is to touch a

59

dozen different patches with a clean finger tip. If any colour comes off on the tip, the gelcoat is not yet set. It is useful to leave test patches of gelcoat in two or three places around the rim of the mould, or one can use the usual accidental drips of resin on the flanges as a tell-tale. If lamination begins too early, with some parts of the gelcoat still wet, the lay-up resin will leach down through it, and allow the glass mat strands to float down on to the mould surface. This gives the finished job a straw-like appearance which detracts from its looks, and in fact allows water into the laminates. Even gelcoat which has just set can be re-mobilised by the lay-up resin, giving rise to this fault. If after several hours the gelcoat has not set, then maybe you forgot the catalyst. See step *12*, page 56.

The reason for laminating the deck first is that if one is using the 'one-piece joint' system (see page 74) it is better to have a clean hole to work through than a wet soggy edge which deposits resin on one's hair. In the method here described, the order is not critical.

18   Mix 4 lbs lay-up resin for the deck
Mixing methods are described on page 54.

19, 20, 21, 22 Laminate deck
Remember—a sense of urgency without haste.

Using a 5″ soft roller, cover the whole surface of the deck gelcoat. A brush is necessary to wet the ends which are too narrow for the roller to enter. Lay the pieces of glass in position, already cut (see cutting pattern, page 50). Ensure that each piece overlaps each other piece by at least $\frac{1}{2}″$. Ensure also that the overlap is well wetted with resin before the two edges are brought together.

Novices tend to put glass in the job, complete with overlaps, and then slap on resin. Resin can make its way down through one layer of $1\frac{1}{2}$-oz mat, but balks at two unwetted layers. The resultant laminate is weak and porous.

Having covered the whole job with one layer of mat, end to end, and round the cockpit area, roll it over with a hard roller, methodically. Use the brush to squeeze the mat down at the ends into the very end points of the deck, otherwise unsightly delamination bubbles will be left there. If the resin is too thick, or the resin-glass laminate is not sufficiently rolled to expel the air, the tiny bubbles coalesce and make large bubbles which are trapped within the laminate, often between gelcoat and glass. These break through soon after being finished, being brittle and without support. They are often found around the joint line and sharp edges like the bow or stern or cockpit edge. Quick work reduces the incidence of bubbles.

Lay-up another layer of mat from side to side just in front of the cockpit and about 18" from the front of the cockpit hole forward. Laminate as before, using a soft roller or hard roller. Examine the whole job, and using the brush take a single brush width of lay-up resin all around the edge of the cast, keeping the waste edge standing straight up. If it is too long, so that it bends over, it must be cut off. Use scissors. If it does not quite reach the edge, then ease it up to the edge with the brush, slightly stretching the wet mat for about 5-6".

Finally, lay on the cloth left over from the hull as a smooth lining all around the cockpit area, and for 12" behind and 18" ahead of the cockpit. Use any spare resin to paint over the cloth.

23 Check lamination and trimming edges on deck
The final job before cleaning the rollers and brushes is to examine very closely the whole cast, as follows:

a   Look all around the edge of the cast. Check that the edge is properly laminated and resin-wet all around, with no dry patches. Check that the waste edge is not so long that it falls over, and delaminates inwards, or bends over on to the flange and causes a referred bubble (invisible) along the top edge of the cast between the gelcoat and the glass laminates (this gives a long bubble in a very conspicuous place on the finished boat, along the joint line).

b   Look around where the knees will go. Is the cloth surface smoothly laid down? Any edges of cloth will leave little spiky bits of glass sticking up, no matter what you do, so abrasives will be necessary to remove the spiky edge when set hard.

c   Examine the stern of the boat, from centre line to mould

61

edge, from end to cockpit. Do it in two sections. Look for resin-wet 'sumps', e.g. along the deck ridge, and use the soft roller to re-distribute the resin. Look for gritty bits trapped under the laminate with ring delamination, and remove them, re-laying the glass. Look for resin-dry areas, and brush a little more on, scrubbing it into the surface with the brush.

d Having done the stern, quarter and search the bow deck section and correct similarly.

e Now leave it severely alone. Any disturbance with setting resin can cause permanent delamination.

24 Clean soft roller, hard roller and brushes
In the case of a soft roller (E), place the roller in a pot of clean cleaner, about an inch in the bottom, and milk the resin out of

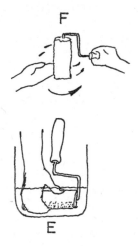

Cleaning the rollers

the soft surface by rubbing firmly with the thumb and fingers whilst slowly turning the roller in the hand. Do this thoroughly, and then hold it away from the surroundings, close to the floor, and spin it vigorously several times (F). This works as a spin drier works and leaves the soft surface ready for the next time.

If there is any hint of colour in the soft surface, do the whole thing again, using clean cleaner again. To be absolutely sure, use a cleaner-soaked rag to finish off, as for the brush (G, on page 58).

The hard rollers should be cleaned at the same time as the brushes, by rubbing the brush along the ribs on the roller in order to clean the resin out of the valleys between the ribs. Be firm with this, as the resin tends to cling in the narrow gap. Finally run the roller in clean cleaner, and spin and shake out the residue and leave it to drain out over the edge of the pot.

It is always better to dismantle the roller and so ensure that the dirty cleaner in the hollow internals is drained away. If not, the roller may be put aside, seemingly clean, and then re-used. The discoloured fluid inside the roller then leaks out and can put dirty-looking smears on to a light-coloured laminate.

See also step *14*.

25 Clean hands with brush cleaner

By the time you have cleaned the rollers and brushes, your hands will be fairly clean. However, some resin will be thickening and setting around the edges of your nails. The nails are slightly warmer than the rest of the hand, so resin will set here quite quickly when you are working. A scrubbing motion with the brushes being cleaned will remove this, but if you are starting, you will be slower when working, so resin will be set quite hard. Use the point of the trimming knife to clean out the flakes of resin, with more of a levering out than a paring movement, as it is rather easy to pare down into the finger nail with painful results.

In addition to gummy hands you will have splashes up your arms, and smears there where you have laid your arms on the sticky mould edge. If your arms are hairy as mine are, the resin really causes havoc if it sets—it is like taking off a sticky first-aid plaster. Take a clean cloth, and slop a little cleaner from the cleaner jar on to the cloth. At once, before it evaporates, wipe your hands and forearms with the cloth. Once is not enough, do it again, and clean between your fingers, and under rings, like my now immovable wedding ring, by twisting the ring around whilst wiping clean. Do not put the hands into the cleaner, as it can penetrate the skin.

If this is the final cleaning, now rub in cleaning paste, and wipe off the surplus on to a cloth. Wash the hands in hot water and soap.

26   Shape footrest flanges and drill bolt holes

In order to determine the shape of the flanges, it is necessary to decide where one's feet will fit in the finished boat. If another boat of the same pattern is available, then sit in it, and mark the point where one's toes touch the deck. Measure back from the bows to this point, and transfer this measurement to the boat under construction. This mark, placed on the flange, shows where the centre point of the flange will be. The further from the bows this point is, the wider will each flange be, and the nearer to the bows, the narrower.

Again, a narrow flange placed nearer to the cockpit will sit lower down in the hull, or a wider flange put nearer to the bows will sit higher up; take care that it is not so high that it obscures the joint line. Alternatively, measure the inside leg measurement of the paddler, then measure that distance from the centre point of the forward edge of the seat, to give the centre of the flanges.

Having obtained the necessary pattern, by trial and error in the first case, mark out a hardboard pattern for further flanges. The two flanges are separated from the flange mould, and the edges cut clean and to size. The two flanges are clamped face to face in the vice, and both filed to a trim outline. A power drill is used to put $\frac{5}{16}''$ holes at $1\frac{1}{2}''$ intervals along what will be the edge not attached to the hull. Before fail-safe footrests, it was necessary to drill these dead accurately. Now it is necessary only to get them about $\frac{1}{2}''$ in from the edge. Set aside ready for use later.

27   Attach flanges to footrest-placing jig

This is a plate of plywood or alloy (see page 65), or even grp. It is drilled with holes so that when the footrest flanges are bolted on the flange edges are ready for laminating into the hull, and when set and the jig removed, the two inner faces of

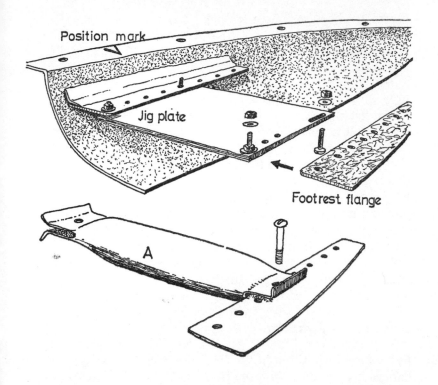

Position mark

Jig plate

Footrest flange

A

Footrest assembly

the flange will be parallel and ready to accept the footrest bar.

The footrest jig as shown in the lower drawing, A, has several advantages over a ply plate. It is very difficult to stick the flanges to the alloy tube, and as no nut is required on the bolt which holds the flange in the jig, that cannot stick either. This jig is only useful with the fail-safe footrest method, as the accurate register necessary to get both rows of holes parallel is not possible. Incidentally, it is possible to fit the flanges *after* the deck has been joined to the hull.

It is easily made from a length of 2″ diameter scrap alloy TV aerial support tubing. Flatten one end almost to the thickness of the flanges to be carried in the ends. Turn the flattened ends up to stiffen the plate, and to prevent resin running into

B

the holes when the flanges are being fixed in place. Measure the required width, and flatten the other end similarly. Make sure that the end slots are parallel, by sighting through the tube. Pinch these in the vice until the average 4-lamination flange is a nice spring fit in the end slots. Pop a bolt through a suitable hole drilled in the end of the jig to hold the flange firmly in place. The flanges should be stiffly held in place, but free to move to line up with the hull taper. It is important to cut the flanges so that this taper is correct.

When the flanges are fixed in place and hardened, knock the bolts up, and pull the jig out with a looped cord.

If each flange is firmly bolted on to a plate jig with two bolts, one fore and one aft, it can be a back-wrenching, neck-twisting job to get the jig out if the canoe has been joined up. Sometimes this is necessary when one wishes to press on with joining up before the footrest flanges have been set in place firmly enough to remove the jig. In that case it is necessary only to enter the fore bolts into the flange holes, without nuts. The nuts of course are necessary on the aft holes which are accessible enough from the cockpit hole.

When bolting on the flanges to the jig, do it so that when the flanges are in position in the hull, the raw, fibrous side of the flanges is uppermost, and the jig plate is under the flanges. The joint is made on the upper surface of the flanges, and if the jig plate is on that side also, there is the risk of spare resin and glass touching the jig, so sticking it to the job.

Set the assembly aside until required.

28   Check that hull gelcoat is ready for laminating
See step *17*.

29   Mix 5 lbs of lay-up resin for hull
It can be 2 lbs if you are unsure of yourself, but more than 7 lbs is not required. The less you mix at a time, the more often you must go and mix up more.

30-37   Laminate hull
It may be better to laminate the hull before the deck, especially if a footrest is being fitted, as the flanges will be set firmly

enough to remove the footrest jig plate before joining up the mouldings.

Using the soft roller, layer the inside of the gelcoat surface all over with lay-up resin. The bow and stern will need a brush. Lay in the first layer of material, the 1½-oz glass mat. Adjust its position by hand, and ease out wrinkles as far as possible. Do not spend more than five minutes on this. Now roll all over it with the soft roller and lay-up resin, covering all bare patches, until the white of the glass mat is completely obliterated with the colour of the resin. White resin laminates are particularly difficult because the colour difference is so small. Work in the bow and stern glass using a brush. If some parts of the glass laminate do not quite reach the edge of the mould, ease them up into place with the brush when the glass is completely wetted out, by stretching the glass slightly over a distance of about 6″ from the edge.

Roll all over, methodically, from end to end, using the hard roller. Work in areas, first all round from the edge of the mould about 4″ down, then across the bottom of the mould, side to side where the bottom curves up to the side, then along the curve, so that the whole area is covered. The whole process so far should not have taken more than 15-20 minutes for one person.

Check any dry areas, and ensure that the upper edge is completely wetted out and laminated to the gelcoat surface. If there is too much waste edge it will bulge or curl, and it must be cut down.

Now put in the wearing patches, about 2″ wide and about 18″ long, at bow and stern. Use the brush to work these in.

Lay on the glass cloth, and shape it fairly carefully with the hands. The best way to ensure a good lay is to stretch it lightly end to end, and get the central threads lying in a straight line. Then smooth it in so that the transverse threads are exactly across the mould in the centre. Now quarter the job, smoothing outwards and diagonally upwards from a central area, keeping an eye on the lie of the threads, so that transverse threads always lie exactly transversely. A brush used more like a squeegee, pressed down firmly so that the bristles bend right back but not so hard that the metal ferrule snags the material, will pull the cloth to the required shape. Folds along the edge *must* be eased out. It is useless to fold them over or to press them down. Again, by quartering and working toward the ends from a central point on the canoe, it is possible to get all the wrinkles out.

Having laid down the cloth neatly, roll it all over repeatedly with the soft roller, collecting surplus resin from any puddles, and re-distributing it on the dry areas. Finally use the hard roller, but do not use anything but firm light pressure. The lower laminate is beginning to set now and hard pressure will crumble the setting resin, leaving the tell-tale dotted or ribbed marks to show where the roller spoiled the resin structure. These marks do not show inwardly, on the laminate; they show outwardly, only to be seen when the canoe is taken from the mould. Translucent boats particularly show these marks. From start to finish, the whole job so far should not have taken more than 30-40 minutes.

Check the lamination and cast edges all over, ensuring that faults have been eliminated before the resin begins to set. It is too late afterwards.

Take the stiffener former, and lay it open side downwards into the mould, along the centre line as far as possible. Now lay over this four 3-ft strips of glass, each 4" wide, so that each piece just overlaps the next by $\frac{1}{2}$". Brush lay-up resin lightly all over the exposed glass, going from end to end in five minutes, not spending any time on any part of the job. Some people pre-wet these strips, but you can work quite well directly on to the job.

Return to the beginning of the strip, and start forming the glass mat, now beginning to soften as it wets through, down on to the former and on to the canoe bottom. Go from end to end quite quickly, say in 3 minutes. Start again, and correct any dry patches on the job, being selective. Ignore the areas already properly covered. Go to the start again, and this time use a hard roller lightly to consolidate the laminate down on to the job. Now go once more over it with a brush and make it neat.

A common impact damage on slalom and white water canoes, is found directly under the forward edge of the seat. The stiffener is shattered, losing its stiffening properties just where they are needed most. So lay in an extra 1½-oz laminate under where the seat will go, over stiffener and all, but there is no need to take this right up to the mould edge. Stop it about 3″ down from the edge. The thickening area should be about 2 ft long, the rear edge being under where the seat will go.

38 Fit footrest flanges

Take the prepared footrest flanges already mounted on their jig plate. Ensure that the coarse threaded bolts nearest the cockpit hole are firmly tightened up so that the flanges are firmly held. The bolts nearest the bow need only enter the hole in the flange. The bolt position may have to be adjusted in its slot in order to register with the flange bolt hole.

Lay the flanges and jig into position, as marked on the flange, with the raw laminated side of the flanges uppermost, jig plate underneath the flange plates. Adjust the angle of the flanges to suit their shape. If the forward end of the flange plates is wider, relative to its position, than the rearward end of the flange plates, then the forward edge of the flanges will ride higher in the hull. This is a good point. If the opposite is the case, it is a bad point. A little adjustment on the jig is permissible at this stage, but the inner edges of the flanges must not be more than ¼″ out of parallel.

Take up the three pre-cut strips for joining each side. These strips are 1½-oz mat, each 2″ wide, not more, and each ½″ shorter than the flange. Pre-wet each one and lay it in position, do one flange, first layer, then the other flange first layer, then the same order again for second layer and then third layer. Take care not to dribble resin into the drilled holes on the flanges.

Sometimes the bolts are not tight on the jig, and the flange plates take up odd angles. By using polythene sheet to protect the polystyrene blocks, it is possible to rough-cut blocks to prop the jig plate into a position so that the flange plates are nearly in the same plane. Fitting the footrest flanges should take about 15 minutes.

39 Trim deck and cockpit hole

This cannot be placed exactly in a time sequence. During all the work that has been going on with the hull, the deck laminates have been setting. From time to time remember to reach across and touch the waste edge standing up all round the mould. If it is soft and floppy still, leave it alone, but if it feels springy, it is just right for trimming. If it is hard and no longer springy, it is going to be a difficult job to trim—in extreme cases, for example if the job has been left for more than 12 hours, it is necessary to remove the casts from the moulds, saw off the waste edge with a coping saw, and to join the casts outside the moulds (see page 78).

The time taken to fit the footrest flanges may be time enough for the hull laminates to have set enough to trim. The factors which dictate setting rates, assuming you have used the proper catalyst-resin proportions, are as follows:

a   Ambient temperature 65°F-70°F, 30-45 minutes.
b   Resin types: some have a long wet stage with a sudden and short green stage, others a short wet stage with a long green stage. The wet stage is called 'pot life' (see page 19).
c   Humidity. A damp wet atmosphere slows setting rates.
d   Ventilation. A gentle air movement to remove the fumes from the mould surface does assist setting rates.

When trimming, cut always toward the flange. Never, ever, cut down on to the mould surface. Take care that the blade cutting pressure is always towards the flange edge, or the cast will easily lift away from the mould, the edge will develop irregularities, and when the joint is made unsightly bulges and breaks on the joint will show.

40   Check lamination and trimming edges on hull
See step 23.

41, 42, 43   Clean tools and hands
See steps 14, 24 and 25.

44   Trim deck and cockpit hole
The deck cast must be trimmed dead level with the flange surface. The edge of the laminate around the cockpit hole should generally be trimmed down to the mould edge, but it is useful when releasing the deck mould from the finished canoe to have

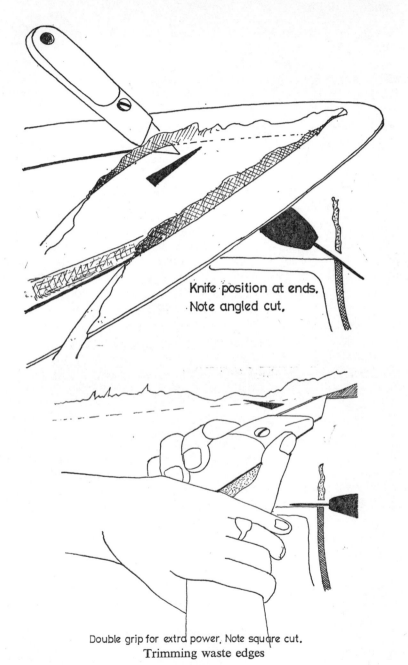

Knife position at ends.
Note angled cut.

Double grip for extra power. Note square cut.
Trimming waste edges

a small lip there on which to exert pressure and so ease the cast free.

45   Check that cockpit gelcoat is ready for laminating
See step *17*.

46   Laminate cockpit
This must be done well, and it must be done with one mix of resin if easy trimming is required. There are two main kinds of cockpit mould, one which is the exact shape of the cockpit, and the other which is like a jelly mould, being a complete shape with no holes in it. The jelly-mould type gives a very sound cast, with no fluffy edges. The trimming must be done with a coping saw after separation from the mould. In the more usual exact-shape mould, the trimming should be done directly on the mould whilst the resin is still green. There is a risk of fluffy edges with this type of mould.

The glass is laid ready, cut according to the pattern. This cast must take all the weight of the paddler during what can be very violent changes of direction. Four layers of 1½-oz mat are usually enough, for an adult-carrying canoe. A junior boat would require only three or possible two laminations of 1½-oz mat.

Wet the whole mould surface with lay-up resin. Lay the seat pan piece on the mould. Paint lay-up resin very quickly, but thoroughly, all over the glass. *Do not work it in.* Next do the side pieces, then the strip around the rim, tearing the glass strip in order to fit it around corners. When one layer is on all over, say after 5 minutes, form it down with the brush. There is no need to be meticulously careful, as an approximation to the shape is enough provided the glass is well supplied with resin. A resin-wet condition is desirable.

Next, lay on the second layer in exactly the same way, working quickly, simply dosing the glass with resin and allowing it to wet out on its own, then forming it roughly into shape after the whole surface has been covered. The third layer goes on next in the same way.

At this point decide whether you can get the last layer on without more resin or not. It does speed matters up if you dose the seat with more resin, but really lightweight construction requires a minimum of resin. At the novice stage, it is usually better simply to flow on more resin, as weight is less important. Experience is required to know whether your cast is resin-wet or not.

Take a small ($\frac{3}{4}''$) diameter hard roller and roll down all the layers at once, working out the bubbles which will have developed here and there. This presupposes that you have worked quickly enough for the resin still to be liquid and capable of forming. If, as sometimes happens with slow working or on very hot days, the resin has gone off before you can roll the job, you have a sub-standard seat using about £1 worth of material. I have simply thrown away bad casts in the past. The seat is where the paddler may have to sit tight, with little movement possible, for up to five or even more hours.

Now use what little resin is left, and brush it on all over the surface. This brushing action, if done lightly just as the cast is beginning to set, can leave a very fine surface, and it ensures that there are no dry patches left.

47   Check lamination and trimming edges on cockpit
This is much as for *23*, but the eye does not see the surface of the cockpit mould as clearly as that of the hull or deck because of the many changes of curvature. The safest way is to ensure that resin is on all the visible glass, even beyond the edge of the mould, that the rolling has been thorough, and that the edges of pieces of glass have been merged into the general shape of the cast and no longer show a firm edge to the piece.

48   Clean brushes and hands
See steps *14* and *25*.

49   Trim hull
See step *39*.

50   Release footrest jig
If you have done the job properly, it is easy to undo the two nuts and to pop the four bolts out with the jig plate. If you forgot this job in its proper time sequence, and so did it later

after the boat is built, there may be resin on the bolt threads and the nuts will come off only after monumental struggles. Do take care to get this right.

51 Bolt hull to deck

It is necessary to do this properly if a good joint is to be obtained on the canoe. Ensure that all flakes of resin are cleaned off the flange, especially around locating ribs and slots, and that the bolt holes are clean; if the nuts are trapped, a smear of grease or wax in the bolt holes will assist easy bolting.

I use the trapped nut system (see page 111). Place four bolts to hold the two moulds together in line. Pop all the bolts into their holes. Use a brace and socket to spin the bolts down firmly. An open-ended spanner will do, but it is so much slower. It should be possible to bolt up in less than ten minutes. Many moulds use free nuts and bolts, often wing nuts, and this takes time to bolt up, maybe twenty to thirty minutes.

Look inside the moulds through the cockpit hole, and examine the joint line internally. If there are only slight gaps, not more than $\frac{1}{8}''$, then the job should be a good one. If as occasionally happens, the trimming was faulty, then the joint may be propped open by raised edges and this shows by quite open gaps in the joint. You can either strip down the bolts again, re-trim and do it properly, or put up with a badly-made joint; the introduction tells you why that is a poor notion.

52 Set out wetting-out board

See under workshop organisation, p 33.

53 Mix 1 lb laminating resin

As described under resin mixing, p 54.

54 Make joint

Three basic methods of joining the hull to the deck are shown.
A is the trimmed edge joint, suitable for two-colour jobs,
B is the wet joint, in one colour only, but with good holding
    power and no waste,
C is the joining strip using 'H'-section extruded plastic.

In each case 1 is the gelcoat, 2 is the first lamination of $1\frac{1}{2}$-oz

74

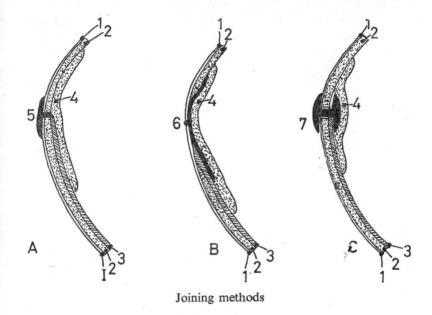

Joining methods

mat, 3 is the second lamination of 10-oz woven rovings, and 4 is the joining strip of 1½-oz mat, common to all.

In A, item 5 is the trim stripe which is applied after the boat is built, and it usually fills the joint gap to a greater or lesser extent. The joint gap is a break in the continuity of the material of the boat, and all stresses must be taken through the joint strip 4. If it is not complete, then seepage may take place along the joint. One layer of 1½-oz mat is enough, as there is no point in using two layers to attach a lightweight deck. If you build a heavy deck there may be some point in using a double thickness joining strip, but you will rarely have trouble with a well-made joint using only one layer.

In B item 6 is a layer of gelcoat applied internally before the joint is made. This work should all be done when the cast is still wet, or green. There must *not* be any spare material above the mould edge when the boat is laid up, no waste edge to be trimmed as in A. The joint, being made green, is much more secure, and the work must be done more quickly. The only drawback is that the boat must be of one colour all over.

75

When the boat is removed from the mould, there is a neat pip of resin all around the joint line, which requires no external trim line; however, a worn mould will have a rough edge which will make for boats with progressively worse joint lines, and these may require trim stripes for cosmetic reasons. For the skilled laminator, and for one who is working alone, this is the preferred method; it is quick, uses less material, and saves time on trim lines with well-cared for moulds. Moulds can soon lose their crisp edge, and the method does depend on accurate cutting and laminating to fine limits.

In C, the two halves of the cast are left to harden in the mould, and are then trimmed and removed from the mould. The plastic 'H' extrusion is then eased on to one part of the boat, and the other part slipped on to it. Inexperienced people have a most frustrating time lining up the two halves. In this case the mould does not perform the second function as a jig for joining up. This means that a mould can be used twice in one day if necessary, but that is cruelly fast work unless oven-accelerated curing is used. When the moulding is in place, and the two halves lightly taped together, the boat is slung up and the joint made in the usual way. This method is mostly used commercially or by people with unsophisticated simple moulds without jig ability for joining.

Have the joining strips ready. Lay half of them over the joined moulds, handy by the cockpit. The moulds should be propped up on edge, with the cockpit hole toward the light. The wetting-out board on a stool or trestle should be on the left of the cockpit hole as you face it. The long brush is ready, and the short brush lies beside the resin pot on the wetting-out board. A torch, or lamp on a wander lead will assist visibility considerably, and long-haired people may wish to wear a bathing cap.

Wet the long brush, and dose each side of the joint with lay-up resin, working from the far end toward the cockpit. About two or three brush loads should be enough. Take about 12″-14″ of joining strip and lay it on the wetting-out board. Dose the surface of the glass at once with a generous amount of lay-up resin, using the short brush. Immediately pick up the wet strip, still stiff because the binder has not yet softened, and drape it over the end of the long brush with about 3″ on the brush head, the rest trailing. The strip is carried up the length of the hull, trying not to drag it along the joint line until reducing clearances make it essential. As soon as the strip begins to drag, it may begin to slide off the brush head, so be quick. It should be possible to drop the strip right on the joint line, fairly centrally, and the 3″ or so on the brush head is forced up on to the upperside joint and worked into the very end, using the brush.

The next lengths are usually 12″ to 18″, wetted with resin in the same way, then laid along the long brush, head and shaft, and carried over the joint, where the strip is dropped on by turning the brush.

It is necessary to have a slight overlap of about ½″ on each strip. If the ends do not quite meet, then you can drop on a very short piece to cover the gap, or leave it and hope the trim strip will cover it, or forget about it until you start sinking through seepage out at sea. The gap may be only ½″ by $\frac{1}{16}$″, but it can accept a lot of water in two hours.

Cover the joint line with strips until within hand reach of the cockpit. Smooth the strips finally, using the long brush from the far end toward the cockpit hole, using a fish-tail action, brush on edge, stroking the glass toward the cockpit hole and outwards from the joint line. If it rucks up, stop at once, and push it gently back into place. The fish-tailing action is a knack, and the natural spring in the extension pole can be used to develop a very neat smooth action, from the wrist.

Now turn everything to the other end and do the other third of the side, using the long brush. The lay-up resin may be close to setting, but the easy part is left to last. Working with the short brush only just inside the cockpit hole, pre-wet the inside of the joint line, lay on strips of dry glass, then wet the whole lot with resin at one go. Leave them to wet out, then smooth them down with the hand brush as described.

The time for one side should be not more than twenty minutes. If the joint is well made, having no dry patches or air bubbles under it, the job can be turned over at once and the other side done. If you are a complete novice, leave this side to set first, then turn it over. The joint on the other side is done in the same way.

77

JOINING EDGE TO EDGE. There are several ways of joining the edge of one piece of material to one edge of another piece. One of the most useful methods is to use slips of alloy material, and to glass over the joint behind. When the mat strip joint has hardened into position, the screws are removed and the alloy slip taken off. This method is useful because it allows adjustments to be made to the alignment of the edges by bending the alloy slip. The slips should be spaced about every 8″ along a long joint.

Cut the necessary number of alloy slips from a piece of sheet about 16-gauge. Use a straight edge and a sharp knife and score the surface of the alloy, and then bend and so break the slips off. The slips should be about 4″ by $1\frac{1}{2}$″. Each slip, or tab as it is called sometimes in this book, is drilled with four holes, the clearance size for the screws to be used, one at each corner.

The two edges are lined up and stuck approximately in place with masking tape. A hole is drilled near to the edge, and one screw put in to hold the first tab roughly in place. The other three screws follow, and the tab adjusted by bending so that the edges are aligned. This is shown in drawing A. When all the tabs have been fixed, cover the remaining gaps with masking tape.

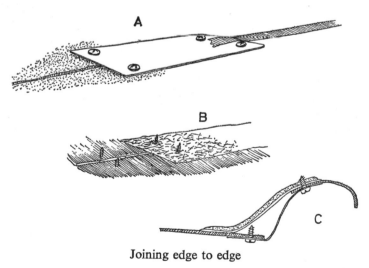

Joining edge to edge

Turn the job upside down, either by slinging the boat or by turning it on the trestles. Take pre-wetted strips of glass mat, wide enough to cover the gap, and form into position over the screw points which stick through on this side (see drawing B). Sometimes, as when fitting a cockpit into place, there is a wide gap to cover. In this case cut a piece of glass cloth, or woven rovings, as well as a piece of mat, and pre-wet and laminate the two pieces together before placing over the gap. The woven material stops the mat from bagging too much (see drawing C).

Later, when everything has hardened, take the masking tape off, remove the screws and tabs, and file the joint line clean. Use filler to fill in the small gaps, but large gaps, as are found with grafting a cockpit into a deck as in C, should be filled with a coarse filler composed of gelcoat and glass mat scraps all stirred together for two or three minutes until a squashy dough is obtained. This is smoothed into position almost up to the final profile required. The final finishing and filling is done with regular filler, such as David's Isopon, P 38. I use a 4-kilo tin for each new design, which is quite expensive, and so worth economising on. Gelcoat is expensive too, but not as expensive as that.

ALTERNATIVE METHOD OF MAKING THE DECK-HULL JOINT. Since this book was begun, I have tried a method of making the joint which was first suggested to me in 1966. It takes half the time, involves a minimum of mess, but it is more difficult for a novice to make a proper resin-wet joint.

Some special preparations are necessary. So far I have used a 2″ mohair roller (A) pushed into the end of an alloy tube. However, some use a sprung wooden clothes peg fixed to the end of a rod, with a wire release to one end of the peg. The alternative idea drawn (B) is to have an alloy tube flattened at one end and turned down. Through it is drilled a hole in which a long wire can run. In use the strip of mat is turned back on itself (C) and pushed on to the protruding wire. When it is in place the wire is pulled out and the strip is released to lie in place. The slight extra length is necessary to go right into the end of the canoe where the device cannot fully go. The brush is used to push it in the last inch or so.

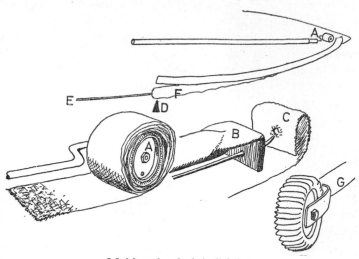

Making the deck-hull joint

Cut a length of 1½-oz mat, 2″ wide and about 6 ft long. This must be cut from the length of the roll, not across it as before. Four pieces are necessary. When they are in place there will be a short gap between the ends of the fore and aft pieces, and this is closed with small pieces suitably cut to length. Place the long pieces against the canoe mould outside, and estimate where the piece must start if, when unrolled inside, it must just reach to the end of the canoe. Mark this point (D) on the outside of the mould, using a pencil or felt pen.

The two halves of the cast, deck and hull (E), have been made in the usual way and the two halves of the mould bolted together. The mould is placed on a trestle on edge, the cockpit opening at about waist level. Mix about ½ lb of gelcoat, colour it to match the deck or hull, and paint it over the joint inside (F), in order both to fill the gap between hull and deck and to produce a sticky surface for the dry joint strip to stick to before being resined down. Do both sides before starting to lay the joint strip.

Take one piece of joining strip, and roll it on to the 2″ mohair roller. Take the free end and hold it just over the point previously marked, where it is to begin (D). Unroll the strip by pushing the roller up the length of the canoe on the end of its extension pole. Just as it reaches the end, the end of the strip should slip off the roller and lie more or less in the very end of the canoe. If it is short do not worry: either put another short piece in or rely on the end block to make that final short length of joint. Do the same for the other end on the same side.

Mix about ½ lb of laminating resin, coloured to match the gelcoat, and fix a 2″ laminating brush into the end of the extension pole. Paint resin on to the joint strip, starting near the cockpit. Ensure that the strip is generously covered with resin with no unwetted white patches showing. Allow the resin to wet out, and meanwhile do the other end on that side. Go back after a short delay, say five minutes, and ensure that all the ruffled bits are smoothed down and all parts of the strip thoroughly wetted out. Now fit in the short closing piece, and wet out.

When the strip is properly wetted out and smoothed into place, turn the whole mould over on the trestle, and at once do the other side.

A well made joint done quickly takes about 20 minutes to complete both sides. A slow joint, such as a novice would make, will take about half an hour for each side. In the first case, it is not necessary to clean the tools between sides unless the workshop is very warm so that the resin is setting quickly. In the second case, always clean the tools between sides, or setting resin will ruin them as you are working.

With the roller method, if you have the tool required it is a simple matter to slip the roller shaft into the end of the extension rod. However, careful cutting of the strips and planning of the starting point is necessary. If using the rod with the spike, the far end of the strip can be carried exactly into place and dropped there. It is easier, too, to lie the strip over the joint line, so one can use a narrower joining strip with less weight.

Some builders take an old roller, cut it in half, and round off its edges to make a cheese shaped roller (G), which can then be used to consolidate the joint strip. This roller is 1″ wide and 2″ in diameter.

55-56 *Make and place end blocks*

Mix up about ¼ lb of lay-up resin in a pot. Take some clean scraps of glass mat, and stir it into the resin. After three minutes the binder will have softened, and the scraps will have degenerated into a mushy dough. If wet resin is still to be seen puddled in the pot, put in more glass until all the spare resin has soaked up into the glass. Do *not* use glass cloth or woven rovings.

Pick up the lump, and pull it into two halves by hand. Any other way tends to be still messier. Lay one half on the end of the long brush and carry it up to the end of the canoe as quickly as possible. It may fall off half-way, but simply prod it into place with the long brush. Puddle the lump about until any entrapped air in it can be assumed to have been worked out. A good firm central thrust usually squashes the dough into the very end, and air comes out along the side of the lump. Carefully form the air-free lump into a neat shape to close the end.

An end block is necessary at each end.

57 *Clean brushes*
See step *14*.

58 *Clean extension pole*

This is really rather important. If it is not cleaned thoroughly the tiny strands of glass fibre become surrounded with resin, and the little spiky ends stick up all over, almost invisibly. The next time the pole is used, someone finds his hands spiked in four or five places with tiny slivers of glass and resin which may make his hands smart; if it was he who left the pole messy then he should have got the spikes in his head—maybe they would make that smart, too. It really is much easier to brush down the pole with brush cleaner, and then to give it a wipe with a cleaner-soaked cloth, than patiently to file off the hardened mess several days later.

59 *Clean hands*
See step *25*.

60 Trim the cockpit

Take care that this is done when the cockpit is ready for trimming. It is put here because this is about when one might expect to find the laminate ready. Test if it is ready for trimming by flicking the waste edge with the finger, and if it is springy it is ready for cutting. Note that the seat may have some extra-thick areas and these will harden sooner, so being too hard for easy trimming by the time the less thick areas are ready. It is useful to leave some small protrusions around the cockpit rim, so that a point to begin leverage is available.

61 Make footrest bar

This simple and effective system was devised in 1971 by Frank Goodman, and there have been at least three drownings in canoes which might have been avoided if this bar had been fitted. Frank's firm, Valley Canoe Products, will supply the bars ready-made quite inexpensively. Alternatively, broken paddle shafts, both in wood and alloy, can be used.

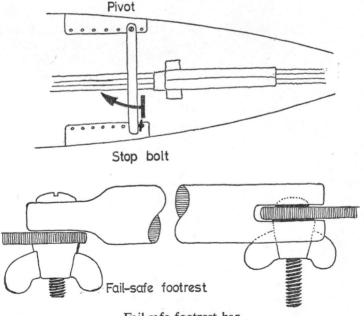

Fail-safe footrest bar

Make the bar long enough so that it will span the width of the canoe without fouling the sides at the forward end of the flanges. A slot just a little wider than the thickness of the flange is cut in one end, and the other end is made to a flattened shape, in the vice in the case of an alloy tube, or with a wood-file or rasp if it is wooden. Drill a hole at one end only to take the pivot bolt.

To fit the bar, estimate where the feet will reach, and put the stop bolt and nut in a suitable hole at one side. Then place the bar in position, and fix the pivot bolt and nut. This can be a difficult job. Ensure that the footrest bar will hinge backwards towards the cockpit easily without snagging anywhere.

In use the principle is that the feet will brace firmly against the bar, and it will be firm against the stop bolt. If there is a violent impact, as in surfing, and the feet slip over and jam behind the bar, it is simple to pull back and the bar hinges free, thus releasing the feet.

62   Check that joining strip has set

If the joint has been properly made it should set hard in about three hours. It can set to some extent and seem hard enough, but when separation of the moulds is attempted, the hull and deck are seen to be moving relatively. That may be because the resin for the joint was not properly mixed, and a part of the strip is not fully catalysed and still wet.

If that happens, put the boat back in the moulds at once and clamp it up firmly again until properly set. Normally leave the boat in the moulds overnight.

63   Remove moulds from deck-hull

Remove all bolts and fasteners. Take the bolster and at one end force it between the two flanges. Do not use a sharp instrument, as this can actually lift the gelcoat of the flange from the flange lamination, and make an unsightly and potentially sticking area on the flange. You may gently knock the bolster into place with a rubber-headed mallet, but bringing any hammer or mallet near to a mould is dangerous, if anyone who lacks the patience to do the job properly is about.

Work all round the flanges, easing them apart with the bolster used as a lever. You should see air slipping between the cast and the mould as you go. Generally the deck will pop off before the hull. The cockpit rim is a usual sticking place. If you have left one or two parts of the deck sticking up about $\frac{1}{4}''$ or less above the cockpit-hole edge, brace the bolster blade against these exposed pieces and jolt inward toward the centre of the cockpit hole and at right angles to the laminate surface. This should separate the deck cast from the mould around the cockpit.

Apply upward pressure at one end, and with the fist clenched muffled in a cloth if necessary as it can hurt, thump the mould at the edge of the internal air bubble. Continue until all sign of adhesion has gone. Now lift off the deck mould and place it to one side, with care (there is a great temptation just to drop it to one side in the excitement of taking out the cast).

Place the hull mould with the cast in it on the floor, making sure that no objects lie under the hull mould. With an assistant holding down one end of the mould, straddle the mould at the other end and with both arms braced down on to the mould flange, one hand at each side, use a series of downward jolting movements in order to start the separation of hull and mould.

Work towards the centre of the boat, then work in from the other end. Sometimes the cast separates at this stage and the boat may be lifted out, but usually, it is necessary to lay the cast and mould back on the trestle, upturned, so that the degree of air penetration can be seen. Again, thump with a wrapped fist around the edges of the separation until the whole cast appears separated. Put the mould back on the floor, and continue.

The assistant holds down the flange centrally on one side of the mould with his foot or hands. Put one foot on the flange on the other side, and with one hand at the front of the cockpit hole, and the other at the back, lift upwards. The cast should now separate from the mould.

If you have a really sticky one, try again. Take a mallet, and place a wooden block on the flange at the very end of the mould at either end. Knock it down firmly but not with any great power, or the flange edge may fracture. Watch the casting flash round the mould edge. If it is seen to move relative to the mould, that end has separated. Take two slips of $\frac{3}{16}''$ plywood, about 2″ by 8″, ease one each side between the cast and the mould, and run these slips from end to end each side. At the end which has been jolted free, apply upward leverage on the casting flash, or deeper under the cast with the ply slip. Jam a thicker piece of wood into the gap. Get your fingers under the end, but take care that the block remains in position, for if the cast springs back into its place your fingers will be trapped most painfully. Press down on the mould flange, and with a steady upward pressure start to ease the cast up and out of the mould. It should pop out.

If the cast resists this sort of persuasion, again put the cast and mould upside down on the trestles and inspect it. Try again to thump the air between cast and mould. If adhesions still show, and will not be moved, try the following, but only on the understanding that you can ruin the mould through lack of judgement.

A piece of tough rubber, about 4″ square (for example pieces of torn padding from the surrounds of a trampoline), is placed over the place where separation is required. Take a hefty rubber mallet, and with the shaft choked (i.e. held close to the head), beat the rubber pad. Observe the separation of hull and mould. Striations, i.e. light-coloured lines, around the edge of the adhering section indicate stress cracking of the mould surface, and you certainly have a sticker—you have just ruined £15 worth of boat and £85 worth of mould. If, however, the adhering piece was simply being super-awkward, the air will penetrate with a loud crackling noise, and the adhering patch will clear. The cast should now lift out.

64   Clean mould flanges of resin flakes

Use a blunt chisel, or a chisel-headed scraper blade. A sharp chisel if used with care will not slice into the flange surface, and it soon becomes blunt enough for less cautious use. Clean especially down into any location holes or depressions in the flange. If the flange was properly waxed before the boat was made, the resin flakes should flick off easily.

65   Wash out moulds with soft wet sponge
This removes any traces of PVA adhering to the mould. Later, when the mould is run-in, there is no need for this, although a mopping or dusting out of the moulds before making the next boat is a good thing. Take care that if the sponge picks up hard resin flakes it is cleaned at once, otherwise the resin flakes may scrape the mould surface.

66   Put moulds away
Place them together, with a bolt at each end and a bolt centrally on each side to stop them slipping apart and perhaps damaging themselves in sliding off their perch. Place them cockpit-hole downwards, so that sharp items cannot lodge in the hull. It helps to keep dust out of the moulds, too.

67   Place hull-deck on trestles
The better way is to have the canoe tilted on its side.

68   Trim flash with file
Trim off the flash by using a milled body file, as follows. If you are right-handed, stand at the left-hand end of the canoe as you face one side. With your right arm holding the file across the edge to be trimmed, and steadying the free end of the file with the left hand, turn the knuckles under the file until they make contact with the shiny hull and deck. Using the knuckles as guides, run the file diagonally along the joint, thus clipping off the flash without allowing the file to scar the surface of the canoe. It should be possible to rip off the flash on one side in less than five minutes. Remember, a sense of urgency without haste.

69   Fit buoyancy blocks
Both blocks are fitted into place loosely, and trimmed to fit better. A carpenter's cross-cut saw is ideal for cutting the material, and a coarse rasp or coarse sandpaper will trim the block very easily. When satisfied the fit is correct, jam the blocks in firmly but not over-tight, or the new and still soft hull can be deformed permanently.

Cut two pieces of $1\frac{1}{2}$-oz mat about 8" by 4", so that the toe

87

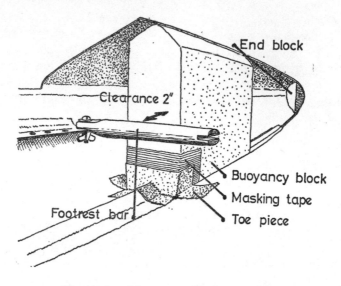

Footrest and buoyancy block assembly

piece, as on the drawing, will fit. Mix about 2 oz of lay-up resin, or better, gelcoat, and using a short extension handle on the brush, work the pre-wetted toe pieces into position.

Not only do the blocks provide buoyancy, but they give vertical support between hull and deck, which gives extra strength to the thin $(1\frac{1}{2}$-oz$)$ decks now commonly used. The block is held in position by a small 'shoe' of resin and glass, one layer only. The drawing shows how. The resin would attack the polystyrene foam unless protected, so it is necessary to use about 4″ of masking tape along each edge to make a cover for the foam.

The block is kept in place by the groove along its base which fits over the stiffener rib, and by the slope of the deck sides above; it cannot go further into the hull because of the taper of deck and hull toward the ends, and it cannot come out the way it went in because of the 'shoe'. Under extreme vibration, as in surfing, the block can shake out and may need to be replaced with a new shoe. If the canoe is very new, still 'green', it can deform the hull and deck if a block is jammed in too tightly.

88

70   Clean brush
See step *14.*

71   Release cockpit from mould
Use a palette knife to ease the front end of the cockpit up from the mould. Better still, use it on edge and knock a slight protrusion of the new cast upwards off the mould surface. Attempting to slip a thin blade between cast and mould will almost certainly result in horrible delamination injuries to the mould. Once the rim has jolted free round the front end, use a bolster and ease that round the rim. Do not force it in the middle. You can help the seat off by dropping the seat and mould on to the floor from a height of not more than 18". The shock springs it loose at once. It should then pop off.

72   Clean up the cockpit cast
Use a coping saw, with a sharp blade, and a 3" disc in the drill to sand off the edges. It is then finished off with a file and coarse sandpaper. Remember that you may be sitting there for several hours, and if what you are sitting in is chafing your skin until it bleeds, you just sit there and bleed—but you see to the rough edges before you go out next time.

73, 74   Fit cockpit
Sling up the hull and deck. See workshop organisation.
   Prepare a low trestle and a wetting-out board as for the deck-hull joint. Prepare two strips of mat, $1\frac{1}{2}$" wide, and 3 ft long. Clamp the cockpit rim into place with four clamps, with the screw heads of the clamps turned inside the canoe. Use little hardboard pads, about 5" by 2" to stop the clamps slipping on the curve of the deck near the cockpit. You will find that the cockpit rim sits better with the clamps one way rather than any other, so experiment until you have the cockpit centrally in the deck hole, not tilted or too far from the hole edge. Mix up about $\frac{1}{4}$ lb of gelcoat, and tear the first strip of mat into a strip long enough to go behind the seat side. Pre-wet this with gelcoat and ease it into place. It is useful sometimes to press this down into the deck-cockpit 'V' joint with a palette knife. Leave it and at once place the other strips round one side of the joint line

89

until the whole of one side is covered with strips loosely in position. Now firm these down with the brush. Speed is essential because gelcoat sets rapidly. With one side done, clean the brush and at once do the other side by altering the tilt on the slung canoe.

75 Clean brush and hands
See steps *14* and *25*.

76 Drill end holes
Put the canoe in its trestles. You can do this straight after fixing the cockpit, provided the clamps remain on. Use a $\frac{1}{4}''$ drill, and drill right through the hull on the joint line, about $1\frac{1}{2}''$ to $2''$ back from the ends. Since there is an end block in place, it will not matter that you are going right through the boat, as you should not penetrate the interior of the hull. Follow through with a $\frac{1}{2}''$ drill, and use a burr or some way of chamfering the edges of the hole to an easy curve so that the end loops when fitted will not chafe through. It helps to have someone on the other side to resist drilling pressures, but keep him out of line with the drill bit, as it can come through with a rush.

77 Trim cockpit-deck joint
If this has been properly made, the edges against the cockpit rim will be standing up with about $\frac{1}{4}''$ of glass showing. If caught when green the waste edge is easy to trim.

The inner edge of the joint should have been well laid down against the inside of the deck with no raggy edges. However, raggy edges may be found, so remove these by cutting them out when green. Take care not to pull out the joining strip, as in the green stage this is not yet quite firmly stuck. Remember that someone's knees may be pressed against the inside of the deck for several hours, and if the sea is rough the knee grip must be firm or kayak control is lost. The condition of knees held in this way against a rough, unfinished deck is a sad sight. When the joint has hardened, say after 24 hours, sand it off smooth, using a coarse sanding disc by hand.

78, 79 Fit seat braces
These are fitted to stop the seat swaying slightly when the canoe

is in use. The slightest movement leaves one with an uneasy feeling that all is not well with the canoe.

Three alternative ways exist: braces between the canoe bottom and underneath the seat: braces between the sides of the seat and the inside of the hull just where the seat turns from the side to the bottom: or braces high up the side of the seat just under the deck.

The bottom brace will be broken out very quickly when used on rough rivers. The low side-braces can also be broken out fairly easily by side blows. The firmest brace of all is the high side-brace. The ease of construction is in inverse ratio to the reliability of the brace.

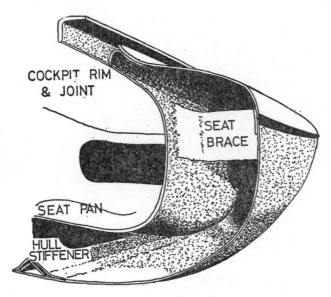

Cockpit assembly

For a high side-brace, make two blocks of polystyrene foam which will just jam in tightly between the seat side and the hull inside, just where the deck springs away. Cover the blocks with strips of masking tape, the thicker the better. Jam the covered blocks into place, about 2″ back from the front edge of the seat side, the canoe being on its trestles.

91

Prepare two pieces of glass mat for each side, about 8″ by 2″. Laminate them with gelcoat on the wetting-out board. Brush gelcoat on to the attachment points. Pick up the wet, double thickness glass strips and mould them into place against the block, the inside of the hull, and the side of the seat flange. Finish off with the brush.

80   Apply trim-line masking tape

Having ensured that the deck-hull joint line is clear of wax, release agent, loose flakes of resin etc. and is well keyed, take a roll of $\frac{3}{4}$″ or $\frac{5}{8}$″ paper masking tape as used in the motor trade. Stick one end of the tape to one end of the canoe, which should be on edge in the trestle. Start the end of the tape about 1″ above the joint line at, say, the front. Run off about 2 ft of tape and pull it into the line required. Form it down 4″ at the end so that it takes up a smooth curve down to about $\frac{1}{8}$″ to $\frac{1}{4}$″ above the joint line, and it lies on the deck section.

With the end 4″ firmly fixed, run out about 4 ft of tape and pull it into line along the joint edge, sighting along the tape with eye, roll, tape and fixed end all in line, the tape held just above the place where it must be stuck down. When satisfied with the line, pat down the tape in three or four places, so that it holds its place without further movement but the whole tape is not yet firmly applied. Do the next 4 ft, and so on until the whole length is taped. Examine it. If satisfied, press the whole tape into place with the thumb and fingers. If not satisfied, lift the tape off and re-align.

The tape is then applied to the hull, and one must get the two tapes as parallel as possible, about $\frac{1}{2}$″ apart. Having done one side, then do the other side. The slightest lack of contact between tape and hull will allow an unsightly intrusion of resin. Take care when inspecting the tape. Aesthetically the narrow line is more pleasing than a wide line (narrow = $\frac{3}{8}$″, wide = 1″). Older moulds tend to have faulty flange edges giving faulty joint lines and requiring more camouflage, so wider trim strips are often found on canoes from old moulds.

81   Mix one side only at a time

Mix 2 oz gelcoat for right-side trim line.

82   Apply right-side trim line

The masking tapes having been stuck on firmly on each side of the canoe, and the gelcoat resin having been mixed, the job is now ready for the application of the trim stripe.

Gelcoat is used because it stays in place whereas lay-up resin dribbles off the job. Also gelcoat usually sets much quicker than lay-up resin. It is necessary, except in a cold workshop, to work quickly.

Brush the gelcoat resin quite roughly over the space between the masking tapes. Be quick and go from one end to the other. It does not matter that some places are missed or that some dabs of colour go over the tapes on to the hull or deck of the canoe. Having gone from one end to the other in two or three minutes, return to the start and take care to cover all the missed places, especially the narrow gap between deck and hull which traps air bubbles that reveal themselves after a few seconds as a clear unfilled gap. It is necessary to use the brush bristles to persuade the resin down into the gap. This second scrutiny should take not more than five minutes. Go to the start again, and brush gently and continuously along the whole length of the job, taking a minute or two.

83   Remove masking tape on right-side trim line

As soon as the trim stripe has been applied, at once remove the masking tape. If you wait until it hardens, as you pull it off it will rip off the trim stripe also, or at least give it a jagged edge. I find it better so to pull the masking tape that it comes off at a constant 90° angle to the canoe side. As soon as the tape is off, go round the smears here and there and wipe them off with a clean cloth, soaked in brush cleaner.

84-86   Left-side trim line
See steps *81-83*.

87   Clean brush and hands
See steps *14* and *25*.

88   Sweep the floor, tidy up rubbish, tidy benches
Take great care that you do not back into the canoe with the

93

setting trim line. Dust is a menace in grp workshops, so wear a Martindale dust mask if there is a lot of sweeping up to do.

Rubbish from the workshop is composed mainly of grp scraps and trimmings, pieces of resin- and solvent-soaked cloth, dust, scraps of cord, old trim-knife blades, broken coping-saw blades, nuts and bolts, screws, pieces of broken bottles, scraps of abrasive paper and worn out sanding discs. *But if you see cigarette ends you are heading for big trouble.* Someone has ignored the instruction 'No Smoking', and *this is highly dangerous.*

89   Put rubbish bin outside

Take the rubbish outside into the open air away from buildings which could catch fire. Either ensure that the garbage disposal crew shifts it very soon, or set light to it yourself. If you do, know that a thick, black, sooty column of smoke will pin-point your fire for up to half an hour, and people may complain.

These rubbish fires are dangerous too, because 'empty' drums of resin catch fire and the mixture of air and resin fumes inside, when heated and ignited, explode, even through the open filler cap end. Soft drink bottles and cans can also explode as the air in them expands in the heat, causing surrounding rubbish to flare out.

90   Check that trim lines are hard enough not to smear

Take care, because if it is not, it will. Some of the trim-stripe resin will have run into the end holes, so it may be necessary to drill these out again before the end loops can be fitted.

91   Fit end loops

A grp canoe is very slippery when wet, and grabbing it in a capsize in a rapid is very difficult. It is helpful to have loops tied to the ends. In order to tie the loops to the ends it is necessary to drill holes in the canoe, and in order that the canoe should not leak as a result it is necessary to put the end blocks in the canoe when building it.

The cord should be synthetic fibre. Laid cord is good, and can be made with an end splice, making a very neat job. However, it is better to use a strong polypropylene cord, about $\frac{1}{4}''$ diameter. The ends are heat-sealed, and then tied with a climber's double knot, or fisherman's knot. The knot should be very firm, as the loop must hold in very difficult conditions or as a suitable anchorage point for lashing a canoe on to a car roof rack.

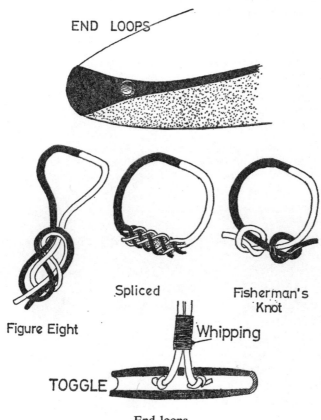

End loops

The simplest possible knot is the figure-eight knot. In this the two ends of the cord are taken through the hole, then pulled together and a figure-eight knot tied in the doubled end.

The loop will usually trail in the water and can be very irritating. Many white-water canoeists tape the loop or knot lightly to the deck with sticky tape, out of the way but ready for instant use.

Recently, to save weight, a simple loop has been passed through twin holes in the deck, and the inside sealed with a grp mat patch.

The end loop system is simple, but it has led to a few accidents, where the runaway capsized canoe has trundled around and around, spinning along its length, and as the cord tightened up the swimmer's fingers trapped in the loop were either painfully squeezed, or even in one case a finger tip was torn off. The preferred method is to fasten a toggle to the end loop. Those obtainable from Valley Canoe Products and Try-lon and several other firms are ideal. One can be made from a length of black alkathene water pipe, $\frac{1}{2}''$ internal diameter, drilled as shown.

92 *Some finishing touches*

a Clean out all the dust and debris from the inside of the canoe so that almost all is removed. Some people find this rubbish irritating to the skin for the first few times the boat is used.

b You can put your 'mark' inside the canoe by writing or typing your message on a piece of paper about 3″ by 4″. Prepare a small mat patch about 1″ larger all round than the paper and, using a tiny amount of catalysed clear gel-coat resin, laminate it to the inside of the hull just behind the seat.

c Clean the outside of the canoe, using a solvent-soaked rag. Polish it either with wax polish, or with a polishing mop in an electric drill and using fine cutting paste.

d When you find you can polish it no more, then stand back and admire it. It really is satisfying just to stand and look at a useful object that you have made. One we made for the 1st Swansea Valley Scout troop was so beautiful, they said they would hang it on the wall just to look at it, but that is going a bit far, especially in view of step 99.

93 *Clean and put away all equipment*

It is astonishing how frustrating it can be to be looking everywhere for a palette knife, and when you tidy up you find it under a piece of rag on the bench you have been using. Good workshop practice dictates that one keeps the place as tidy as one can.

94   Clean hands thoroughly
See step 25.

95   Cleanser cream on hands
Rub in hand cleanser cream, and you will feel it become liquid in a few minutes, as it rubs into the skin. As soon as this happens, and having cleaned around the fingers and any rings and up the wrists, wipe any surplus off at once with a clean cloth. The cleanser removes resin traces from the hands, and is slightly caustic. It will sting the face if it touches there, and if cleanser is left on the hands for an hour before washing off, the skin will tingle for a little while after washing.

96   Wash the hands in hot water and soap
Use a nail brush. Dry the hands well, and by now any sore patches on the hands should have been soothed and any slight rash should subside. If it does not, you are one of the few people who are sensitive to synthetic resin, and you should seek medical advice if the rash has not gone by next day.

97   Record details
It doesn't seem to matter when you start, but if you make a lot it takes on a meaning beyond mere facts: a record of styles, and of people long gone to other things.

98   Use it
You may of course be some off-beat interior decorator, but all this work is for one object, to experience the fun, danger and wildness that is out on the water. As you sit reading this, the sea thrashes the cliffs and caves of Anglesey, the tide races thunder round Ramsay, creaming surf shakes the beaches of Devon, and rivers far from the sea scatter over rock and torrent. Ullswater glints in the sun, and out there the far Bermudas ride.

Canoe Building

99   Knock it about a bit

You will hate to get the first scratch on your beautiful boat, so make haste to collect a few slight grooves in the hull, and a few chips off the ends and trim stripe. You will experience what is near to physical pain, but persevere. Make it more comfortable, put in some fittings, and make a few repairs.

100   Enjoy it

Having disposed of the new-boat-twitch syndrome, enjoy your canoeing.

*   *   *

Variations

A SEMI-LIGHTWEIGHT CANOE. This lasts two years on average,

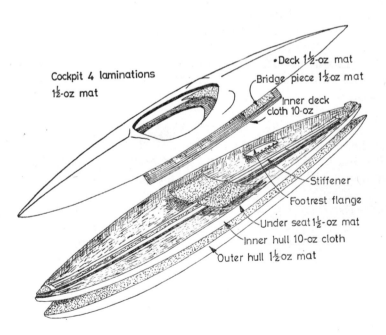

Cockpit 4 laminations
1½-oz mat

•Deck 1½-oz mat

Bridge piece 1½-oz mat

Inner deck cloth 10-oz

Stiffener

Footrest flange

Under seat 1½-oz mat

Inner hull 10-oz cloth

Outer hull 1½-oz mat

Cutting pattern for semi-lightweight canoe

and can always be sold for at least the cost of the material. It weighs 30 lbs plus or minus 2 lbs. The more skilled one is, the less the boat tends to weigh. Too much resin used to build the canoe is a usual beginner's fault, but it is a good one. If a beginner uses too little, the boat will not be fully wetted-out, and it will be porous and weak.

There are certain points to note.

1   The hull is a composite of one layer of $1\frac{1}{2}$-oz mat and one layer 10-oz cloth, and this gives about a $2\frac{1}{2}$-oz lay-up.

2   The deck is one layer of $1\frac{1}{2}$-oz mat with local thickening and stiffening.

3   The joint is one layer of $1\frac{1}{2}$-oz mat, as it is pointless to use a heavy joint to attach a lightweight deck to a semi-lightweight hull.

4   There is a double layer 'bridge' in front of the cockpit as this is where the weight of the rescued boat is taken during tipping out.

5   To delay the onset of leaks through the impact holing that one gets between the bottom of the canoe and the lowest points of the seat pan on which one sits, one can build in an extra lamination directly under the seat.

A LIGHTWEIGHT CANOE. I would never bother with this lay-up, but top competitors, and those who think they can emulate them, usually try for an ultra-lightweight. If you are in that class, you are probably wasting your time reading the book, because the top canoe builders will already know you and your ability and will be doing all they can to get you to paddle their canoes. If you are not that well known, you are probably not that able, and you must perforce finance your own mistakes— ultra-lightweights can be expensive, and very much a mistake the first time you misread a rough river. The lightweight cutting pattern follows.

1   The material used is 1-oz mat and 10-oz cloth.

2   The deck is one lamination of 1-oz mat.

3   The cockpit is three laminations.

4   The joining strip is very narrow, which requires building skill.

5   The hull ends are not always completely double thickness. If the boat has a shortening of the inner cloth laminate, so

that it does not quite reach the ends, then the boat will float, but the first rock it hits will reduce it to shatters.

6   The end loops can be attached to two holes in the deck, and this does away with the need for end blocks. After all, if the bow and stern are so weak, what is the point in putting solid blocks there?

7   The resin used is necessarily of high quality, and of a certain consistency, and the resins which the commercial people use are well-guarded trade secrets. Certainly general purpose resins are not good enough.

8   Brushing on the gelcoat is good enough for all but really light canoes, and an ounce or two can be saved by using spraying techniques to put the gelcoat on. This requires specialised equipment and skill and special resin, again, which only the top commercial firms will have.

9   When the canoe is finished, do not expect a life of more than a couple of months of the usual treatment that slalom canoes must put up with. Too many, far too many, young men plunge all their hard-won savings into an ultra-light-weight, and several months later are sadly wondering what to do with the shattered remnants.

CARBON-FIBRE REINFORCEMENT. The new wonder material was all the rage in 1970. However, it was quickly found that although a super, ultra-light canoe of 18 lbs could be built, it cost a great deal, and the carbon-fibre 'cords' were so stiff that stress concentrated along their edges, and that the reinforced canoe would tear along the dotted line. The use of carbon fibres has just about ceased in lightweights, because of this stress concentration fault. When a carbon-fibre cloth can be produced at a price that canoeists can afford, then the 10-16 lb canoe may become a reality.

SYNTHETIC FIBRE REINFORCEMENT. Terylene and nylon cloth has been used to make canoes for a long time, especially in the USA. Their resistance to impact is usually much greater than that of glass. A new material, polyester cloth, has been in use for several years in the USA and on the Continent. Amateur builders can obtain the material from some manufacturers, at a price about twice or three times that of glass cloth, but this will come down as demand increases. The trade name of this material is Diolene or Diolen. You may have realised that polyester is what the resin is, so the boat is simply all one material. However, it is difficult to trim unless it is caught at just the right time, so not only is great care in construction required, but also a resin with a long green stage and short pot life, which implies the ability to build quickly enough to beat the resin used. The Diolen is used in the same way that glass cloth is used. The boat weighs the same, and has extra strength.

Chapter 4

Moulds

There are two kinds of mould, the female, or hollow moulds, i.e. deck and hull moulds, and male moulds, or convex moulds, with the shiny surface outside, on which are cast such items as cockpits and seats. Recent practice in firms which offer moulds for sale is to make a master mould, which is really two halves of the canoe, quite separate, with the flanges cast on. Moulds are cast from master moulds, and then canoes can be cast from the moulds.

Obtaining the mould is fairly simple now. Various possibilities exist. These are:

1 Copying exactly an existing canoe—'pinching' a mould (see pp 115-16)
2 Taking an existing canoe, altering it, and making an 'altered pinch'
3 Hiring a mould
4 Copying a hired mould
5 Making your own original design. See chapter 5.

Choosing a mould
There are many criteria which affect choice, and some of these are dealt with in chapter 2 of my first book, *Living Canoeing*. To deal with this fully would require about half a book on design problems, so my best advice to you is to read *Living Canoeing* and to join a canoe club, use club boats for a season, and then make up your mind what you want.

A canoe has certain sizes, i.e. overall length, beam, and depth. It may be one, two or four seat. It may be big and bulky or small and neat. The surface can be mirror-like and dead level, or rough and rippled. It can be rippled and brilliantly polished, which only serves to highlight the ripples. The earlier designs made by amateurs were usually not as well finished as those made by professionals, but the pros would not as a rule allow their moulds to be used by amateurs. This is now changed, and as amateur canoe designs approach professional designs in standards, the number of designs with poor surface shape is declining, and some top pro canoes are now available.

Any canoe has three basic forms of rotation, and three forms of stability. It can rotate in a horizontal plane, and turn to left or right. It can turn over along a longitudinal axis, either down right or down left. It can loop end over end, or pitch as the nautical term has it, as it rotates about a transverse axis.

Directional stability is the big problem that beginners have to deal with, and rudders and skegs help. Tipping over seems to be less of a problem these days, and looping is a characteristic that surf gymnasts positively encourage.

You can, by looking at the boat, make a rough appreciation of its points as follows:

1 Length. Longer means straighter running, faster, bigger capacity, slightly more stability in rolling. 17 ft for a solo is long, 14 ft standard.
2 Width. Wider usually means slower, greater rolling stability, perhaps more manoeuvrability and greater carrying capacity. 24" beam is about standard.
3 Depth. A shallow canoe is 10" deep at the front of the cockpit, a deep one is 12" deep there. The deeper it is, the greater the carrying capacity and the more buoyancy it will have in rough water.
4 Profile. If the bottom is heavily rockered, i.e. curved up from the middle to the ends, it will turn easily, it may not loop so easily. It will be slower than a boat of equal length and beam with a straight-running keel.
5 Section. If at the widest point it is flat-bottomed and slab-sided it will be slow, difficult to turn over, and difficult to

roll up. If rounded it will be fast, easy to turn over, and it won't have much carrying capacity. If it is 'U'-shaped it will probably be a reasonable compromise.

6   If it floats high on the water it won't be much good at sea, for the wind will blow it around.

7   If it is one of the small baths boats, about 8 ft long, it will fit inside an estate car and will be great for fun canoeing, surf and polo, but you won't go far in it, as it is slow.

Physical examination of moulds

When you select your mould, look for the following points:

1   Is it from a reputable firm? How do you know? I can't say which are not, as the law might have me! Experience will inform you.

2   Look along the mould surface against a spot source of light. Move your head to examine the surface. Do ripples show? Dull patches? If they do, the finished canoe will also be dull and imperfect.

3   Is the outer surface of the mould stained with resin drips? If so, it isn't new.

4   Is the edge of the mould along the flange cracked and broken? If it is, it has been flexed too much, or used badly.

5   Is the edge of the mould round the cockpit rim chipped and cracked or cut into?

6   Is the flange less than $\frac{3}{16}''$ thick? Is the mould around the cockpit area less than $\frac{1}{8}''$ thick? Does the whole mould weigh less than about 60 lbs (for a slalom solo kayak)? If each of the three foregoing points show, it is likely to be a lighter mould than is useful for good practice. A good mould should have a lay-up (see glossary) of about $4\frac{1}{2}$ oz, usually three layers of $1\frac{1}{2}$-oz mat.

7   Are there bubbles just under the surface of the mould along the flange edge? If there are, these will break down and spoil later canoes from the mould.

8   Is the surface star-cracked? If so, it has been banged with a mallet too hard, and the star-cracking will mark the canoes.

9   Is there any form of external stiffening on the mould? If

there is, look inside at that point and see if the inner surface has buckled, which will be shown by a wavy highlight. Some frames are applied to stiffen the mould, especially if it is lightweight, and careful work will not harm the mould. Personally, I prefer an unstiffened mould, as the flexibility allows the cast to be pulled out easily.

10   If the pair of moulds together, hull and deck, weigh much less than 60 lbs, say about the weight of a heavy canoe, then they are likely to be lightweight, and the surface will ripple and buckle in course of time, about a year or so. Even a perfectly surfaced mould will develop surface irregularities if not built heavily enough.

If the moulds seem perfect, then the full asking price, usually half as much again as a commercial canoe of that design, should be paid. If the mould is second-hand, it is inadvisable to pay more than half price for it, but that depends on what is wanted, and how old it is. If it has had not more than ten canoes out of it, and is not more than six months old, and the condition is near enough as new—no blemishes—then pay up to half the new cost. If there is star-cracking or chipped edges or serious scratch marks (any scratching of the mould surface is serious), then pay about a quarter of the new cost, and either run the moulds into the ground or build a new plug at once, and make a decent set of moulds yourself.

MAKING A SET OF MOULDS FROM A PLUG

It is assumed that you have a properly prepared plug ready for use. A temporary flange has been attached (see pp 133-37) and you are ready to start making the mould. The sequence of events is as follows:

(NB: This sequence is not as detailed as that for canoe building. Mould building presupposes some existing skill in the matter.)

1   Plug ready, flange attached and sealed
2   Coat of release agent all over deck and flange surface
3   Coat of clear gelcoat all over deck and flange surface
4   Strip of 1½-oz mat all round flange, with lay-up resin
5   Strip of mat all round deck side as above

6 Another layer of mat all round flange surface
7 Three 'strings' of rovings round edge, flange-deck
8 Bridging strip, flange-deck
9 Two strips round cockpit hole
10 Three laminations over bows
11 Three laminations over stern
12 Three laminations round cockpit
13 Three laminations between bows and cockpit, and stern and cockpit
14 Trim flange and cockpit
15 Turn plug and half-mould over
16 Remove temporary flange, make good any holes
17 Laminating sequence as for deck, except that hull is covered in one
18 Drill holes, fix nuts and bolts, trap nuts
19 Sand edges of flanges, remove bolts, separate moulds from plug
20 Polish and run-in moulds.

3 Coat of clear gelcoat all over deck and flange surface
It will be necessary to correct a new mould from a new plug, so a good even thickness of gelcoat is required so that cutting down into it will still leave enough material to be polished. Once you cut down into the glass strands, a straw-like surface must result.

If you doubt your ability to cover a surface thickly and evenly with gelcoat, then cover it twice, using two ordinary thin coats, evenly applied. It is a fault to ladle on the resin so that it collects in a thick beading all round the line where the flange springs away from the plug. A thick resin edge here will be pure and brittle resin with no fibrous backing. In use the mould will quickly crack and shatter along the edge, mould surface to flange surface, thus giving a faulty joint requiring much smoothing and filling.

4-9 Reinforce flange and cockpit hole edge
The mould requires to be slightly flexible, so that when the cast is being released from it, the slight flexing allows easy separation. Some manufacturers use glass on wooden cross-

sections, which stiffen the mould and help to keep its shape but which reduce the ease with which moulds can be separated.

A good mould will retain the flexibility of the mould surface by being about a $4\frac{1}{2}$-oz lay-up, i.e. three layers of $1\frac{1}{2}$-oz mat. The stiffness of the mould will be largely supplied by stiff flanges, so these must be made thicker than the mould surface laminations.

Assuming that the gelcoat was applied correctly, and that a thick bead of gelcoat did not form around the plug-flange line it is possible to feed in glass to this edge so that when it sets the edge is firmly braced with glass fibre closely under its surface. The drawing shows what is necessary.

It is tempting to attempt to cover the deck surface and flange surface in one go to reduce the work required. All that you will achieve is a long bubble along the flange edge which will very quickly break down leaving a really bad mould edge. The build-up as described is the minimum necessary for good work.

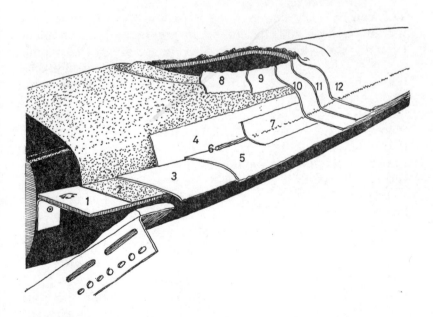

Lay-up sequence for mould building

Canoe Building

It is possible to build a lighter mould by using only two laminations for the mould surface, but it is unsatisfactory. The mould flange should be about $\frac{1}{4}''$ thick when finished.

Referring to the drawing, the sequence is as follows:

1 Flange ready
2 Gelcoat all over
3 First strip along flange
4 Second strip along deck side
5 Third strip along flange
6 Three 'runs' of rovings, slightly twisted
7 Bridging strip
8 First cockpit hole reinforcement strip
9 Second cockpit hole reinforcement strip
10 First lamination all over
11 Second lamination all over
12 Third lamination all over.

14 Trim flange and cockpit

This can be fairly simple or it can be complicated. If you are working quickly and efficiently there will be no problem about trimming the flange waste edge; simply take a very sharp knife and cut along using the temporary flange as a cutting edge. The double-handed grip may be necessary, and it is a job for a strong man's hands.

If one is working less quickly, as is more usual with people who have little experience with laminating, then the first job, that of laminating the four sets of strips around the flange, will have set quite hard before the main bulk of the mould surface resin has gone off hard enough to cut. It is then very difficult to trim, as the earlier layers are just right for trimming but the later layers are so wet with resin that they pull and tear and are impossible to trim effectively. Alternatively, by the time the later layers are ready for trimming, the earlier layers are far too hard.

There are two choices. The first is to trim the lower layer with a knife from underneath. This cuts the set laminations but simply pushes up the wet layers. The later layers are trimmed in the usual way. It is necessary to reform the laminates into

108

position with a brush after cutting out the lower layers. The second choice, probably the better one with a new mould and plug where the temporary flange may not have a neat edge, is to leave it until set hard, then to cut the waste off with a coping saw after the flange has been removed.

15-16   Prepare plug and flange for second part of mould
The plug is turned over when the deck half-mould has set. The screws holding the tabs to the plug are removed, and the temporary flange is prised away and laid aside. The screws are removed for re-use, and the alloy tabs recovered, but the hardboard flange is waste and should be thrown out.

The newly cast flange is then cut if necessary, until it is an even width all round the plug. Care must be taken not to press downwards or the still quite flexible flange will start away from the plug, leading to later problems such as bleed-through of resin to mark the new mould and spoiled registration of deck and hull moulds when finished. The cut edge of the flange is then smoothed with a coarse sanding disc or body file until it is smooth. It is good practice also to run with coarse sandpaper, hand-held, round the sharp edges of the flange to remove any last traces of spiky pieces of glass which can hurt the hands when working with the mould.

The screw holes left when the flange tabs were removed may have raised edges, and a touch with a file will cut them down. The hole is then filled with wax or Plasticine. Slight marks will show on the finished mould and each boat afterwards on this pre-production mould.

The whole is now given one coat of polish over plug and flange surface, then one coat of release agent, and it is ready for casting.

17   Laminate hull
The sequence is as before, well, almost. The release agent having dried, the gelcoat is applied as before all over plug surface and flange surface.

The flange strips and rovings are applied in the same way except that there is no cockpit hole to be concerned about.

Cut a piece of mat to the full width of the roll and about 3″

longer than the plug and flange, measured end to end. Lay this piece right over the plug and form it roughly round the flanges, which are wet with unset resin. Cut roughly round the flange edges with a sharp knife, and put the spare pieces to one side for use later. Peel back one end of the glass from the plug, exposing half the plug surface.

Wet the area with laminating resin on the soft roller, and lay back the glass into place. Do the same at the other end. Work this first laminate very carefully into position, using the soft roller then the hard roller, and brush it round the flanges as all air bubbles must be out of the first layer. Air bubbles in subsequent layers are not important.

Continue on the second layer as for the first, then use the spare pieces, which are mostly triangular, across the mould, fitting them together and patching up the third lamination.

18-19   Finish mould flanges and remove moulds
When the second half of the mould has set, probably overnight, finish off any trimming necessary. The edge can either be sawn off or, if caught earlier, cut off. Go all round with the sanding disc or body file, and make the edges of the flanges trim and parallel. Some resin drips down during construction, so these 'stalactites' of resin must be trimmed off the lower flange too.

Mark off at roughly 1-ft intervals all round the flange and about 1″ from the inner edge of the flange a series of drilling points for holes. Have a complete set of nuts, bolts and washers ready for use. Use $\frac{1}{4}$″ Whitworth bolts, as these have a good coarse thread which makes for rapid bolting up of the moulds and which are easy to clean if resin gets on to them. The bolts are lightly greased, either with grease or wax, but the outer surface of the nuts must be clean. Swill them around in a jar of clean brush cleaner to clean them.

Holes are drilled all round the flanges, using a clearance drill for the bolts in use. Insert the bolts, washers and nuts so that the washer is under the bolt head. Tighten them up firmly but not hard. Mix up about $\frac{1}{4}$ lb of gelcoat and any glass mat scraps into a dough. Using the fingers, pull out blobs of dough and go all round the exposed nuts (uppermost) sharing it out. Then go round and form the dough round the nuts and flanges. Leave the dough to set hard.

When all has set hard, go round the bolt heads with a brace and socket wrench and remove the bolts and washers, putting

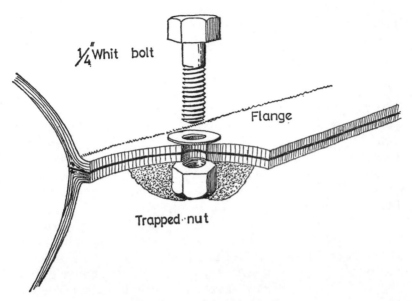

Trapped nut for flange bolts

them into a box ready for reuse. It is a good idea to work grease into the holes and the trapped nuts at this stage, so that wear and tear and loss of register on the moulds will be delayed.

Take a bricklayer's bolster (two preferably) and, with help, insert the bolster blade at one end between the flanges. If your trimming of the mould edges has been correct there will be no problem, but if an overlap has been left this can key on and prevent separation until it is removed. With the blade firmly jammed between the flanges, walk round the flange, sliding the blade along about a foot, working it up and down, then going on again. Air separation will be seen progressing between mould and plug, but it will not be complete.

Go to one end when the flange has been separated all round,

111

and with an assistant applying upward pressure at the other end, start to thump the mould with a clenched fist wrapped in rags. The air should progress further. Work on isolated patches of non-separation until the whole area is no longer adhering. The hull mould should lift off easily. The deck mould will probably require persistent work around the cockpit hole area.

When the moulds have been released, the plug is removed and the two parts of the mould bolted together firmly, being left on edge for up to a week before use.

20 Polish and run in moulds

The sequence for running in a set of moulds is described on page 114. With a brand new set of moulds, there are important points to watch. Resin sets over a period of up to six weeks. Oven-curing can reduce this time, but this is unusual with canoe moulds. The mould should stay on the plug for about 48 hours at least, then the moulds can be separated and the polishing begun. However, as soon as the moulds come off the plug, they can be distorted temporarily and permanently. Temporary flexing is not important, provided it is not extreme. One sees the supports on the trestles pushing in the surface of the mould, but as long as care is taken when polishing that too much is not removed from the surface of the mould over this bump, then no harm will follow.

If, however, the mould is left overnight like this, a permanent distortion will be found, so after a period of polishing, say an hour, bolt the moulds together again to preserve the register of the edges, and then in order to avoid distortion from supports, either sling the mould up using cords hanging from a beam or prop it up on edge in the trestles. Do not leave it flat anywhere. After it has had one day on one edge and the first polishing, polish it again and sling or prop it on the other edge; keep this going for at least a week until the mould is firmly set and truly hard and no longer susceptible to distortion.

*　　　*　　　*

The 'Second Generation' method of mould-making
Take the plug and rub it down with a hard block using 40 to 60 grit 'production paper'. Sometimes an orbital sander can be used, which is not demanding in terms of physical effort but is much slower than hand rubbing. The whole surface is now smoothed down but lined with many scratches. Rub it down again thoroughly with 180 grit wet and dry. Some areas may need filling up to profile, and some bumps may be cut down using a body file. At this point surface irregularities are imperceptible to the eye, but very perceptible to the palm of the hand, which is run to and fro over the area being checked. Hollows for filling can be ringed with a felt pen, humps for cutting back cross-hatched also. Very careful working is not required. The surface is now cut with many fairly fine scratches. Give it one coat of polish and one coat of release agent, fit the temporary flange for the mould, and cast the mould, scratches and all.

All the indented scratches on the plug are now raised ridges on the mould. The single coat of polish and single coat of release agent are quite enough to release moulds from plug. If the surface of the plug is true, then start rubbing down the mould surface using 360 grit wet and dry to begin with, then 600, and then even 1,200 grit if you like. If the surface feels rippled, then cut it down again with production paper on a hard block, and work up the surface, 60 grit, 360 grit, and 600 grit wet and dry. In either case the amount of time spent in rubbing down the slight ridges on the mould is far less than the time spent in filling and cutting the plug with fine wet and dry.

A boat is made from the moulds and tried out thoroughly. Allow several weeks before making the second generation plug. Now cast another boat from the moulds, using two thin layers of gelcoat of medium colour and two laminations of 1½-oz mat, and alter it in any way required—cockpit position, balance etc. Take this plug, and starting with 600 grit wet and dry, and then perhaps 1,200 grit, cut and polish the surface with great care. Put the plug back in the moulds, and then work as for mould copying (page 105). The second set of moulds should not be cut with any paper, but mould running-in procedure (page 114)

H   113 should now be used before that final showroom glitter can be achieved. Even then, the Boat Show model will have been subjected to hours under the polishing mop to get that wonderful finish.

Running in a set of moulds
A newly made set of moulds must be run-in, much as a new car engine must be run-in. The sequence of events is as follows:

1   Polish with mould wax. *Do not use polishing mop in a machine.* The polishing must be meticulous, and by hand. There are several kinds of mould wax. They are all wax based and they *must not be silicone-based.* Silicone allows the resin to leach through and so attack the mould. There are quite cheap carnauba waxes which give an effective finish but a coarse surface, compared with the expensive 'Mirrorglaze'. This is not cheap, is pleasant to use, and one tin lasts for a long time.
2   Leave for at least six hours, then hand polish again.
3   Leave for at least six hours, then hand polish again.
4   Apply mould release agent (PVA) by using a soft sponge and wiping on firmly. If it tends to blob together and bubble off, then rub all over again.
5   Make the first canoe.
6   Clean up mould flanges etc, and mop out with a wet sponge.
7   Polish once again, using mould wax.
8   Apply mould release.
9   Make canoe number 2
10 Repeat stages 6, 7, and 8, and make a canoe each time until 6 canoes have been made.
11 Use cutting and mould glazing paste (mould cleaner), usually a proprietary brand is best when formulated for grp work; 'Formula C', from Valley Canoe Products is very good. This is used to cut down the surface wax of the mould, almost down to the raw mould again. The best method is to use a polishing (calico, 5″ by 1″) mop in an electric drill. Do be careful, if the polish and the cleaner are made by the same firm, that people do not pick up the 'Mirrorglaze' mould glaze and cleaner in mistake for the

'Mirrorglaze' mould wax. The moulds may have a brilliant polish, but the wax polish surface will be completely removed and so the cast will be stuck firm to the mould. That was a £100 mistake which made our bonfire the most expensive in Oxford last 5 November.

12 Repolish three times, stages 1, 2, 3, and 4.
13 Make seventh canoe.
14 Repeat stages 6, 7, and 8 each time until canoe number 12.
15 Wax once and polish, with no release agent; take out canoes 13-20 without polishing again.
16 Polish once only every 8-10 canoes.

The ethics of mould-copying

If you copy a mould, you are taking advantage of another person's experience and hard work, without his consent usually, and so one could say reasonably that mould-copying is a dirty deed. There are degrees in this. From really villainous copying to innocent copying, the scale runs roughly as follows:

1 Commercial firm pinches another firm's design, altering it slightly
2 Small club pinches a design for its own use only, then finds the mould popular and starts to make money with it.
3 Small group pinches a design, possibly unwittingly, and uses it in a small way to develop canoeing in that area, usually for youngsters, and keeps it small and uncommercial
4 Club borrows commercial mould on hire, and copies it without firm's permission
5 Club borrows commercial mould on hire, and copies it with permission.

Generally a small group, such as a school or youth group, if it copies a mould will probably not do much harm to the commercial firm in lost business, and probably in the long run all commercial firms benefit because many more people are being introduced to real canoeing, and some of these will become keen canoeists and will want the best commercial canoes available. Out of these a few, very few, will want to design their own canoes and be able to do it.

One of my designs is being pinched in New Zealand. The

person pinching it even had the nerve to ask me how I thought it could be improved! I call that an innocent pinch, and good luck.

Chapter 5

Plugs

There are many ways of making a solid shape from which moulds may be taken. It can be made of almost anything that will withstand the pull of setting resin and glass and filler. Any canoe, almost, can be a plug, but few plugs can be canoes. It depends on how they are made. Even copying plugs, used for turning out copy moulds, are usually built heavily, and so do not make good canoes after service as a plug. Some of the ways of making a plug are:

1. Spine, frame and timber planking
2. Cross-frames on a base board, with rubble and clay infill
3. Using panels from other canoes
4. Concrete hollow moulds and a plastered surface
5. Spine, frames and plywood or cardboard panels.

If you think number 2 seems ridiculous, it was a little, but it worked, and that was how the first BAT came into being in Wolverhampton on 11 January 1967. All these methods I have used. The fifth method is the quickest and possibly the least difficult. The method of construction follows.

Construction

The necessary drawings must give cross-sections at stated intervals. Allow for the thickness of the skin to be applied, usually $\frac{1}{4}''$ all round, and trace the frame shapes on to $\frac{1}{2}''$ blockboard. Cut the blockboard frames out, and number them in order.

Obtain a piece of straight-grained deal, about 3" square and

117

as long as the canoe. Each of the frame shapes is marked with a central square, and this is cut out so that each frame can be threaded on to the spine, preferably a tight-push fit. Each frame shape must have a gunwale mark and a deck line and keel line mark, so that each frame can be lined up with the next. Neglect of this precaution may lead to inherent twist in the plug which is very difficult to remove. Some armatures are made so that they have protruding ends which rest in brackets which allow the whole thing to be turned over as work proceeds. The protruding spindle ends are cut off just before the plug is ready for mould making.

The frames are threaded on to the spine and placed on their proper places. Four long laths are used as stringers to line up the frames from end to end, being lightly nailed on to each frame, using the marks on the frames for alignment.

Obtain sheets of $1\frac{1}{2}$-mm ply, or even heavy cardboard from a supermarket, and cut panels to fit between the laths. Place the panels and use a heavy stapling machine to staple the panels to the frame edges. When all the panels are fixed, ignore the end shapes, and pull off the four stringers. You can cover the gaps with more cardboard, or you can leave them open as you wish.

Turn the raw plug upside down on trestles and drape glass cloth or mat all over it, trimming this roughly to shape at the edges. Leave enough spare to wrap over the gap where the stringer was on the gunwale line. Roll on resin with a soft roller. If a staple gives way and the cardboard pops up, bang a few more staples in right through wet resin, glass and all. Cook it with a fan heater, and when it is green turn it over and cover the other side.

The cloth and resin when hard gives a firm base on which to build up a 3-oz laminate of glass mat. Do this, rolling thoroughly. Leave it to harden and examine carefully.

At this stage you should have a dust mask near, because the rest of the work is very dusty.

You will note that there is no cockpit hole, and the ends are rough. Cut right across the ends, but leave the spine intact, to obtain a clean end. Take polyurethane-foam blocks, and stick these together with laminating resin and masking tape until

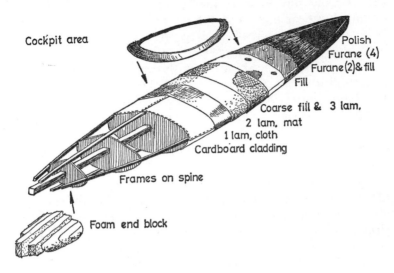

Cockpit area

Polish
Furane (4)
Furane (2) & fill
Fill

Coarse fill & 3 lam.
2 lam. mat
1 lam. cloth
Cardboard cladding

Frames on spine

Foam end block

Plug construction

they form a block the right size and shape for each of the ends. Slot these blocks over the end of the spine, and carve them to shape with the sanding disc.

Every deck has a hole in it where the cockpit fits. All you need to do is to transfer this hole from the old canoe to the new canoe. Cast a section of the deck from the existing moulds, including the cockpit hole and a piece of deck about 3″ wide all around the hole. Trim this, and place it on the new plug where it is to go. This is a time for discussion, because once it is fixed it is fixed. Correction of a balance fault caused by a badly placed cockpit is very difficult later on. It will be central laterally, but longitudinally it must be placed with some knowledge of the likely balance of the new boat. Usually the centre of the cockpit is behind the centre point of the canoe. When it is placed, draw around it on to the surface of the new plug and cut out very carefully with a pad-saw. Graft the old cockpit hole into the new deck using alloy tabs, etc.

Mostly the raw armature will be close to the required shape, but some large depressions will be seen. Mix up about ½ lb of

119

gelcoat, and mix in glass mat scraps until a thick dough is obtained. Smear this on to the depressed areas, using a putty knife. Work at it until all the large visible depressions are filled but not overfilled—this mix is difficult to cut down when hard. Note that if you have skimped on the cladding of the raw plug, these hollows when filled will be pulled into a deeper hollow by the slight contraction of the dough, and so the hole seems never to fill. In that case, overlay the depression with three laminations of mat and take these laminations well beyond the edge of the depression. Leave them to harden for a day or two, and start again.

Use a coarse sanding disc when the plug is really set, say after a week or two, and cut the whole thing down, cutting off all bumps but leaving any hollows alone. This stage gives a rippled feel to the plug, and if final filling is done on this surface the resulting job is badly rippled, a sure sign of an unsatisfactory job. The quality of this cutting down can be improved by bolting a framework of slotted angle material to the drill, giving a crossbar about 12″ long at a reach of about 14″, so that the spinning disc is restricted in tilting either way. In use, one steers the crossbar, and no weight is put on the disc. This reduces rippling a great deal, but it is not eliminated.

After this cutting back, reinforce any thin areas, fill any depressed areas, and cut back again in due course. The body file is less likely to clog than the coarse sanding disc. Clogged discs of industrial quality can be cleaned of resin dust by leaving them in clean brush cleaner overnight or even for an hour during work. Do not put the rubber backing pad in as well.

There are various kinds of filler:
1   Chalk powder mixed with laminating resin to a stiff dough makes a cheap bulky filler, but is difficult to cut with tools
2   Slate dust gives a fine slate-like solid when mixed with resin
3   Flour gives a soft filler which cuts fairly easily
4   Proprietary brands, of which I find David's Isopon P 38 the best. It is easy to cut, sets very rapidly and saves lots of time, if time is at a premium.

Mix the filler in small quantities as it sets very quickly. Wipe the filler all over the deck surface, filling in hollows and wiping clear of high spots. When the deck has hardened enough, in an hour, turn the job over and fill the hull. Inspect with care, run the hand over the roughly-filled surface, and using a milled, flat body file, cut back any high spots.

When this is done, again fill any low spots. The palm of the hand is a very accurate judge of this inequality. The whole job is a dusty one by now, and some may prefer to wear dust masks to reduce nasal and bronchial irritation. Again file off, using a body file and a coarse sanding paper called 'production paper' —either 40 or 60 grit is about right. Use it on a hard block so that the high spots are cut back without low parts being touched. By now, the surface is becoming very close to true, but it is a slow job. After thorough sanding of the high spots, go all over the surface and find the high and low spots remaining, and the numerous little crevices, and remember them or mark them with a marking pen.

Once again, for the third time, go all over the job filling in wherever filler is required. Again, file and sand. When satisfied with the job (or more usually bored rigid with continual tedious hand-sanding), mix up about half a pint of furane resin, and give the whole boat one coat. Give it two if you wish. It dries very rapidly, but it takes 24 hours to harden. The resultant black surface is slightly glossy, which helps the eye in sighting along the plug for any wobbles in highlights reflected from a spot source of light some way off. Investigation with the hand reveals the cause of these variations in the highlights. Again, use filler where necessary. When satisfied, sand all over with production paper. The contrast between the grey filler underneath and the black furane on top, when cut back by sanding, shows up the high spots very well, and is as accurate as two coats of furane are thick. By now you are nearing the end of the first part of making a plug.

When any final filling has been done, apply the final four coats of furane, waiting half an hour between applications. Do the deck one day and the hull the next, otherwise the supports on which the plug rests will mark the surface badly. After it has hardened for at least 24 hours, the finishing of the plug begins, work 180 grit wet and dry, 360, 600, medium and fine cutting paste on a mop, three coats of hand-applied polish, release agent, a temporary flange, (see page 133) and then the moulds. The moulds then receive any final cutting back and shaping before the final production plug is cast and the production moulds are run-in.

Allow six months for this at first, but a plug can be produced although rather rippled, in three weeks.

Making a smaller canoe from existing moulds
In order to make a new type of canoe it is necessary to make the required shape, and then to make moulds from that shape, and then to make canoes from those moulds.

In order to make the required shape, called the plug in canoeing grp terms, a basic armature or core is required on to which the necessary parts are built, e.g. the right cockpit.

It is assumed that you have a good canoe design available, and a set of moulds from which to work. Perhaps a junior version would suit the needs of your group. For example, many scouts are between 10 and 14 years of age, and a full-size canoe can be a burden to them whereas a smaller scaled-down canoe would suit them very well.

Certain basic thinking is involved—very simple arithmetic really. Suppose we reduce the linear measurements of a solid object to $\frac{3}{4}$ of what they were. Length is now 12 ft (say) instead of 16 ft. The change in volume of the object is proportional to the cube of the change in the linear dimensions. A rule of thumb measurement would give the weight-carrying capacity of a canoe which had been scaled down to $\frac{3}{4}$ as being $3 \times 3 \times 3$ to $4 \times 4 \times 4$, or a fraction $\frac{27}{64}$, which is less than half. In other words a canoe suitable for carrying a 14-stone total load, if scaled down by $\frac{3}{4}$ would then be suitable for carrying a total load of 14-stone $\times \frac{27}{64}$, or 5 stone $12\frac{1}{4}$ lbs. That would be suitable for most children up to 8 years old.

Working backwards, what we want is a scaled-down canoe which will carry about 6 to 9 stone, say 8 stone average for a youngster 8 to 14 years of age. Reducing a canoe suitable for a 14-stone total load by $\frac{5}{6}$ (linear) will give a scaled-down load of 5^3 divided by 6^3 of 14 stone, which is 8 stone $1\frac{1}{2}$ lbs, which is just about right.

Therefore a solo touring canoe 14ft long, 24″ in beam and

12" deep, would be suitable for scaling down by $\frac{5}{6}$ to provide a junior touring canoe to much the same overall shape, but its length would be 11 ft 8", beam 20", depth 10" and it would carry 8 stone.

The method of working is as follows.

OVERALL BEAM. This is the first consideration; 4" must be taken out of the width of the canoe. The easiest way is to cast both deck and hull but to miss out the middle 4", i.e. 2" each side of the centre line (hull) and centre line (deck). The cockpit shape will be ruined, and this must be cut out anyway. The overall length of these two halves when joined together will be much less than the original length.

Using masking tape, with polythene sheet between, mask out the central 4" wide stripe both on the hull mould and the deck mould. Note that the hull centre strip is almost flat anyway but the deck line, if sharply sloped to a ridge, will be affected by this slope. However, we are not working to dead accurate measurements now, and the odd quarter-inch does not matter.

OVERALL DEPTH. Reducing the beam of the canoe will not affect the hull depth much, but it will affect the deck depth (measured from the gunwale line). The overall depth is to be reduced to 10". The deck will lose $\frac{1}{2}$" in height with taking out 4" centrally, so between 1" and $1\frac{1}{2}$" must be lost from the hull. Mask off a strip on each side, between 1" and $1\frac{1}{2}$" down from the edge of the hull mould. This must be done completely from end to end.

OVERALL LENGTH. With whittling something off the beam and something off the depth, the total length of the smaller sections will be less than that of the full-size canoe, but it will still be more than what is required. Measure from tip to tip of the masked areas on the moulds. This may be 13 ft in a mould for a 14 ft boat. Scaled down the total length is to be 11 ft 8", so another 1 ft 4" must be lost from the total length. Allowing 2" for cutting and chopping about at the ends when constructed, the total now reduces to 1 ft 2". Mask off a central area taken across the width of the hull and deck moulds in the cockpit area, or in the case of a boat with its widest part in some other place, usually aft of the cockpit, cut out the excess length equally each side of the widest point.

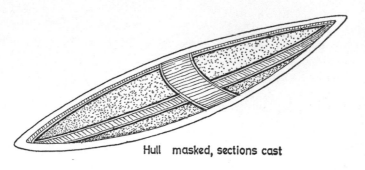

Hull   masked, sections cast

Masking a mould for canoe shrinking

CASTING. You now have a matched pair of moulds, polished, and masked off ready to cast the following parts for your new canoe armature:

Hull: forward left, forward right, aft left, aft right.

Deck: forward left, forward right, aft left, aft right.

That is eight separate pieces which will be joined up to make the armature for a smaller canoe. Laminate in the usual way with a rather thick gelcoat and two laminations of $1\frac{1}{2}$-oz mat.

It is useful to colour the resin a dark blue or mid-grey, as later on when filling out the armature to make the plug the highlights show better on a dark surface. White is confusing when checking highlights, and black seems too dense. Clearly, do not laminate areas you will not require, and remember that the cockpit must be completely altered, so do not cast a neat cockpit—simply stop laminating about 4″ from the cockpit rim measured in any direction. It does not matter if you fail to make enough deck to join to the hull just by the cockpit, as some cutting and fitting will be necessary anyway.

When the eight panels are cast, leave them to set overnight, and then pull them out of the moulds. Pull out the masking tape and polythene sheet and clean up the moulds, as odd drops and beads of hardened resin will be on parts which were not masked off (it pays to mask off thoroughly first). Repolish the moulds, and lay in polythene sheet all over to protect the mould surface.

124

TRIMMING PANELS. The cast panels will have on them the traces of the edge of the masking tape. Cut carefully to this line using a coping saw. Many people lack the steadiness of eye and co-ordination of the hand necessary to cut a neat straight line; slight wobbles are acceptable, but variations of more than $\frac{1}{4}''$ overall do lead to problems. The cut edge can be trimmed with the sander later.

JOINING UP. Take the pieces as follows:

1   Join bow hull right and left
2   Join stern hull right and left
3   Join bow deck right and left
4   Join stern deck right and left
5   Join fore hull to aft hull
6   Join fore deck to hull
7   Join aft deck to hull
8   Fit cockpit section.

The joining up of the hull and deck sections is as follows. Having trimmed the two pieces required, lay them in the fore hull, and as far forward as is necessary to keep them in proper relationship for angle of keel etc. Tack the two pieces together on the inside with four or five pieces of masking tape across the

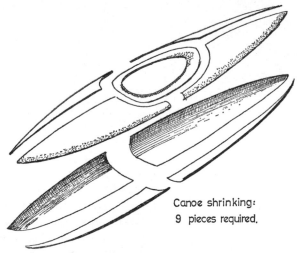

Canoe shrinking:
9 pieces required.

Panels required for canoe shrinking

joint. Lift the two pieces out and tape right along the outer line of the joint using masking tape. Replace in the hull mould. Take out the few tacking pieces of tape. Join along the section with two layers of $1\frac{1}{2}$-oz mat. The method is the same for stages 1 to 4 above. The spare resin drips are caught by the polythene mask in the mould. Leave overnight to harden.

Take the four sections now made, and clean up the edges and joint roughly with a disc sander. Identify the exact centre of the hull casts, which is on the keel line. Mark this point on the inner surface of the fore hull and aft hull casts. Offer up the two ends, and see if they are about the same size around the joint. If they are not, then try to centralise one with the other using the marks made. Take two pieces of alloy slip, 1″ by 4″, and using self-tapping screws link fore and aft halves of the hull with the tabs just below gunwale level. It is essential to keep the keel line true at this stage so, before attaching the second tab and after attaching the first tab, lay the assembly on a bench, and line it up on a line on the bench or with two strings, one above the other, from stem to stern. Having aligned stem and stern laterally, it is now necessary to establish the final rocker of the craft.

Lay the assembly on a flat bench or floor. Block up the ends with anything handy, for example polystyrene off-cuts, and view it from the side. Decide the amount of rocker required, having an eye to the gunwale line. If the gunwale line was straight before, then keep it that way, as the complications involved with altering the gunwale line are considerable. Reducing the amount of rocker involves putting a negative sheer on the gunwale, and this is displeasing aesthetically. An increase of rocker increases gunwale sheer, but this is less displeasing. Now fix that rocker by putting in an alloy tab across the floor of the two parts of the hull inside. This should fix the two parts in relation to each other.

Turn the assembly over on a bench and, starting from the keel centre line, work outwards tacking one half to the other with alloy tabs, working on the outer, polished side. The tabs should be placed about 2″ apart, trying always not to allow any bulging between tacking points. Remove the very first two aligning tabs after the first three tacking tabs have been applied.

Carry on until the two halves of the hull have been lined up and firmly tacked together. Turn the hull over, hollow side uppermost, and remove the third aligning tab. Make a glass joint, using two layers of 1½-oz mat. Work well round the projecting screw points, as these will screw out anyway later. Leave to harden overnight, then remove the alloy tabs and clean up roughly with the sanding disc. You can speed up everything by making a 'tent' and blowing in hot air from a fan heater. A night's setting can be done in one hour in this way.

The ends of the rough hull armature are really raggy usually, with no shape as yet, but ignore this at this stage.

Take the fore deck section, and offer it up to the fore part of the hull. Tape it roughly into position with masking tape. Look at it carefully, and make any adjustments now, such as cutting a slip from the deck edge in order to reduce beam or deck height still further. Use alloy tabs to tack deck to hull, one at each side of the bow and one at each side of the cockpit end. Take care not to introduce a bulge on one side when working with one tack so far from the other. Use masking tape generously. Now go right round using tabs every 8″-10″, halving spaces, i.e. if the two ends are fixed, next fix the middle, then the middle of each of the two resulting spaces, and so on.

Join the foredeck to the hull in the usual way, but make the end block particularly generously in order to have plenty to cut at when shaping the end. When this is hard enough, then attach the rear deck to the hull. Leave it overnight, then remove all tabs and clean up the joints externally with the sanding disc.

COCKPIT. It is now necessary to consider the cockpit. You can, if you have a number of cockpit moulds to use, simply choose that shape which suits your needs best. However, you may need to make your own cockpit and seat. If you choose a full-size cockpit as for the full-size boat, this saves time and it leaves you with a canoe with a disproportionately large cockpit hole, useful for easy exit for the novice but a curse for the improving canoeist who wants to stay in his canoe on rough water. If this is your first venture, then there is no need to try fancy variations on the cockpit rim—use the existing rim unmodified. Go to your original deck mould, and cast a piece all round the cockpit hole about 4″ measured all round. Laminate this as for the hull and deck sections. When it is hard, remove it from the mould, trim and clean up, and offer it up to the hole in the rough armature. Wedge it in place *under* the existing deck hole, using polystyrene off-cuts etc. Adjust it for position so that it is central laterally, and so that it is within an inch of the required longitudinal position. This is done by referring to the seat to be used, remembering that the centre of gravity of the average canoeist is about one-third of the way from crutch to knee-cap.

Having decided the position of the cockpit hole, fix it using six alloy tabs, two each side one fore and one aft.

Now sling the assembly upside down at head height, and work inside the cockpit. Ignoring any bulges or misalignments, simply span the gaps between the cockpit piece being grafted in and the deck inside with pieces of glass cloth about 6″ square. Wet these well and lay them in place as roughly as you like, but these pieces must not protrude above the eventual deck surface. When this is hard, drop pieces of pre-wetted mat into place to increase its strength. Leave them to harden, then take the boat out of slings and clean off any resin drips and rough pieces of glass. Set the whole thing up on a trestle, and look at it with great care from all angles. It is often worth leaving it like this for several days and brooding on it from time to time.

FINAL FILLING. The shape is by now impressed on your mind, and the shape you want can be seen in the armature you have built. Certain typical faults will show. The transverse joint in the hull and the gunwale line at the mid-point joint will be out of alignment. The ends will be raggy and of no shape at all. The area around the cockpit rim hole will be full of depressions and odd bulges, symmetrically disposed each side of course. Using a coarse sanding disc, cut the gunwale line back until the curvature looks right—sighting along the gunwale line is useful here. Take care not to cut right through the joint, so thicken the joint internally if a great deal of cutting back is necessary, in order to have a sufficient thickness to cut down into. Similarly adjust the keel profile. Clean up the ends and cut deeply if necessary as there is a good thick end block to cut into. Cut out any extraneous bulges around the cockpit hole.

Now look for all the holes you can see. There will be many gaps to be filled, most of them quite small and insignificant. However, there may be one or two big holes with something underneath them to stop the filler simply going right through. The filler I use, David's P 38, is too expensive to waste, so I mix up about ¼ lb of gelcoat, and stir in mat scraps until a thick dough it made. I then place this in the holes and trowel it off level using a putty knife. When this is set the surface is cut back using a sanding disc.

The armature is now taking shape. Using P 38 the surface holes are all filled as neatly as possible. This is usually done in several stages. The filler sets hard within 15 minutes at average room temperatures, so do not mix more than 2 or 3 oz at a time. By the time you have worked from bow to stern filling all holes, it will be possible to go back to the bows and cut back the filler using a body file. Some small holes will still be left, so again fill these. Cut these back, and again leave the job for a day or two and brood about it. At this stage you can add or remove knee bulges, deck ribs etc—in fact your final decisions are being made. It may even be out of line, and you may need to decide to cut it in half again and join it up with greater care. The 'dies' are about to be cast.

Making a larger canoe from existing moulds
On this occasion there is no need to mask any surface, as the hull will be cut along its length centrally and an insert put in; increased depth is unlikely, and increased length can be achieved by cutting the boat in half after joining up and inserting a piece. Several tricks of the trade are used. The method to make a double from a single is as follows:

Taking a 24″ beam solo, to increase its beam to 27″ requires the introduction of 3″ in the bottom as a 3″ wide strip along the keel line, end to end. The deck is treated differently. Cast the hull, but do not cast the bow 6″ or stern 6″ of length. In fact the hull is an open-ended casting.

Make the deck pieces. Do not cast the cockpit area. Simply cast the stern deck and the bow deck to within 4″ to 6″ of the cockpit.

Obtain a mould for the cockpit required. Cast two cockpit

I

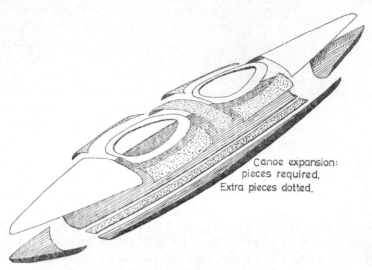

Canoe expansion:
pieces required.
Extra pieces dotted.

Panels required for canoe expansion

areas from the solo mould, allowing a 4″ to 6″ skirt all round.
Lay these aside to set, and trim them for use later.

Take the deck and hull sections out, and repolish the moulds.
Cast two ends for the hull as dictated by the overall length
required and the beam at the open ends of the hull section
already made. The complete end pieces of the hull are
to be grafted on to the open-ended parts of the hull in due
course.

Cut the hull lengthways along the keel line, using masking
tape to give the line required. Take long pieces of hardboard
or alloy sheet, and screw the two halves of the hull together to
the hardboard or alloy. Use loops of cord to hold the two
halves of the hull in proper relation to each other. Cast two
thicknesses of $1\frac{1}{2}$-oz mat internally across the 3″ gap. Set the
widened hull aside.

When the hull has hardened, trim the ends square and clean,
and offer up the fore deck to the fore end of the hull; there will
be a foot or two of overhang at the bow, because that part of
the hull is missing. Tape and tab the deck section into place,
and glass it on. The same system is used for the stern. When

130

these are set, clean up the exposed edges and graft the hull sections, bow and stern, into the overhung deck. Cut and fit these into position. The flat-bottomed centre section of the hull will not match with the 'V' bottom of the bow section, for example, but later filling will overcome that. The bow and stern sections will match at the gunwale line only, but the centre section of the hull will take a greater girth at the joint than the bow and stern sections.

When this has hardened and raggy edges have been trimmed, fit the two cockpit areas into place, loosely, taking care that longitudinal balance is maintained. Try to have not less than 30″ of deck between the rear of the fore cockpit and the front of the aft cockpit. Closer than that and the paddling actions of the paddlers interfere with each other; further than that and the rough-water performance of the boat is reduced (on the fly-wheel principle—mass towards the ends, and the rotational inertia of the boat is increased, thus increasing the time necessary for the ends to rise to waves and making for a wetter boat that ploughs through rather than lifting).

Of course, as the cockpit deck areas are fitted into place, the bow and stern deck sections will have to be cut out to accommodate the new parts. The area between fore and aft cockpits is completely missing at present. Glass the cockpit decks into place.

Take a sheet of aluminium slightly larger than the deck area missing between the cockpits. Alternatively it could be big enough to cover half the area, with the deck centre line for the joint. Curve the alloy sheet as nearly as possible to the required deck shape. Screw it into place with four or five self-tapping screws. Remove the screws and place the alloy sheet on the bench. Wax it but do not polish to a shine. Do not use gelcoat, but simply laminate two layers of $1\frac{1}{2}$-oz mat on to the alloy sheet on the inside of the curvature. Whilst this is still wet, screw the sheet back into position, and turn the armature upside down so that the alloy sheet is underneath the boat, to ensure that the laminate keeps down on to the sheet and does not separate and so lose the shape.

When the assembly is hard, remove the screws and sheet; the new deck pieces can be shaped and fixed from inside, and the

131

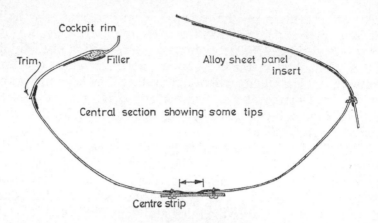

Joining methods for panels

whole filled and smoothed, as described before. The mould-making method is as described on page 102.

Plug finishing
It has been said that the plug should receive a super polish and that all one's efforts should be made towards that end. However, money and time come into this decision. You must decide if your time is worth more than the cost of materials. The criteria are as follows:

A dimple on the plug will become a pimple on the mould. Further, surface 'ripples' are common on first plugs, and can be worked out of the mould as a hollow on the plug becomes a hump on the mould. In this context a hump and a hollow may be no more than $\frac{1}{8}''$ measured perpendicularly to the surface plane.

Quality is important. To work on a plug with care and then to cast a mould, and again to work on that with care, then to take a plug from those moulds and make a second generation model, having tried out the boat from the first moulds, is to get a pretty true plug quickly. However, it costs a first generation boat which may be wrong and which is certainly not well finished, it costs a set of first generation moulds which are good but not very good and which may produce boats which do not

132

perform well enough, and it costs a second generation plug and a set of second generation moulds. Roughly the extra cost of working in terms of a second generation set of moulds, with all that implies in terms of time saved, improved finish and a tested boat to work on, is between £30 and £45. Time saved and quality proved is the reward.

However, to work up a first generation plug and mould to a good surface will take perhaps four times as long as the second generation method, and can be frustrating to the man who has already spent several months on the job, especially as you still do not know if the thing will perform properly. The cost here may be 40 hours extra work, with a lack of performance data and quality dubious. I now prefer to use the second generation method, and to sell the first generation trial boat and the first generation moulds for the cost of the materials to replace them, a good enough bargain for many impecunious groups.

A temporary flange for taking a mould off a plug
The method described here is simple and satisfactory. It also informs you how to copy any canoe that you may have. Ethical and legal considerations enter here. The method, however, is essential if one is to build a set of moulds from a plug.

It is assumed that the plug is quite ready for copying to begin. The surface is highly polished, and prepared for moulding.
1   Stretch ¾″ masking tape into position along the chosen joint line. The upper edge of the tape is the line to which one will work. It is much easier to use paper tape in this way to establish a line, as if it is not correct it is quite easy to lift it off and re-position it. Using a marking pen to determine the line is possible, but the line is as wide as the felt nib, and thus not exact; also the black marking ink does not show very well against the

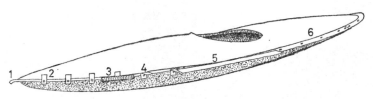

Temporary flange

(usually) black plug. Both sides are taped before the tabs are attached. Check-measurements from the centre line or gunwale line are used to make the joint line symmetrical each side.

2   Make about 18 alloy tabs for each side of a 14 ft canoe. These tabs are of soft alloy, about 12 to 16 gauge, and about 1″ by 4″. Cut the tabs from alloy sheet, using a straight edge and a sharp trimming knife to score the alloy. A few bending movements cause the strip to come clean away along the scoring line. The tabs are clamped into a vice, and a single $\frac{1}{8}$″ hole put through, about 1″ from one end of the tabs.

3   The tabs are now screwed into position all round the joint line, by first drilling $\frac{1}{8}$″ holes (or whatever size hole is necessary for the screws to be used), and self-tapping screws put in. The holes go in just under the lower edge of the tape. Accuracy in placing these holes is not necessary. They should be about 9″ apart, give or take an inch or two. I use the screwdriver overall length as a makeshift measuring stick. The tabs stand up above the joint line.

4   Go round the tabs, and using a strong straight edge, such as a body file, turn the tabs over. The upper edge of the file should be exactly along the upper edge of the tape marker.

5   Pieces of good-quality hardboard are prepared. These should be about 3 ft long, 4″ wide, and $\frac{3}{16}$″ thick. Surface quality is not important—it can be new, painted or even quite rough. The better the surface, of course, the better the job. These pieces are offered up to the joint line, resting on top of the turned-over tabs. Make an alloy scriber frame as illustrated

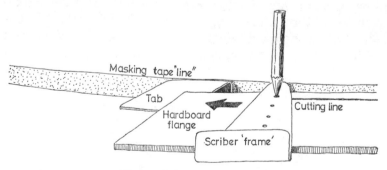

Fitting flange pieces to canoe

and scribe a line on the hardboard, parallel to the curve of the joint line, while a helper steadies the hardboard. The outer edge away from the joint can be left quite rough, as the final trimming of the flange will be done on the glass and resin cast. The end pieces are usually made from pieces of hardboard shaped into a 'U' piece, and then fitted with care. A tolerance of up to $\frac{1}{4}''$ can be allowed when fitting the inner curve of the hardboard to the curve of the joint line.

When scribing the line on to the hardboard piece, the hardboard must not alter its position in the slightest, and the scriber frame must be kept at a constant angle to the plug.

6 The piece is now cut out, using a coping saw along the curve of the scribed line. It is again laid over the bent tabs, and held in place while one screw hole is drilled at one end. This goes through the piece and the tab underneath. One self-tapping screw is then put in, head showing on the surface of the hardboard, point down into the tab. With one end fixed, the other end can also be fixed with a screw in the same way and then the intermediate points are screwed down. If the tabs are close together, say 6'', the hardboard will be held in a very close line to the joint line required. If they are further apart, the accuracy of the joint is compromised. I work to 9'' centres between the alloy tabs. Joints between the ends of adjacent pieces are arranged over a common tab, otherwise it is necessary to insert intermediate tabs to carry the joint. In the case of pointed-end canoes, the end pieces are usually made from a rectangular piece of hardboard 12'' long and 6'' wide. A 'V'-shaped slot is cut in the end, and the pieces continually offered up and then trimmed until the fit is correct. It is assumed that the side flanges end about 3'' away from the very end of the canoe. If this type of work is new to you you will probably waste a few pieces, but hardboard is cheap enough so persevere.

Having now fixed all the hardboard flanges into position, go all round the plug and the flange checking that the flange is nowhere less than 2'' wide, and that nowhere is the gap between the inner edge of the flange and the plug more than $\frac{1}{4}''$. With skill you can usually get it to around $\frac{1}{8}''$ by noting places where the flange touches and by sanding them away, reducing the high spots and so making the whole job a snug fit. However, once the screw holes are in, it is impossible to alter the position of the flange without drilling new holes.

Finally, one must make the surface of the flange as neat as possible and close completely the gap between the flange and the plug—if this is not done, resin dribbles through on to the plug under the flange and so causes problems when the second half of the mould is to be made. A quick way to do this is as follows: Stick the main part of a piece of masking tape down on to the flange along the edge nearest to the plug, and so arrange the lie of the tape that about $\frac{1}{16}''$ lies on to the plug. Take care when pressing this to the plug that you do not press it down through the gap, and thus 'lose' it. Having gone once round the flange like this, continue working outwards with strips laid parallel until a width of two inches on the flange has been covered with paper tape. This covers all screw heads and gaps between adjacent flange pieces and will give a mark on the first cast flange to which one can cut, thus making a good neat flange for the mould.

Alternative ways exist in which to close this gap, and one can do this with mould wax pressed into place with a putty knife or with Plasticine similarly applied. In order to stop the material going right through the gap, it is necessary to tape over the gap under the flange. I now prefer the method described in the previous paragraph.

The whole flange is now waxed. As a high polish is not essential, the wax is simply smoothed on but is not polished off. A final application of release agent all over the upper surface of the flange and the plug is all that is necessary before the mould is cast. When the first half of the mould has been cast and has set, the plug and half-mould are turned over and the screws holding the temporary flange are removed from the plug. The whole flange is then peeled off from the newly cast and hardened mould flange. The screw holes in the plug are filled with wax, and the paper tape which was first applied as a marker is peeled off. If it has been trapped into the half-mould, simply slice along it neatly with a sharp knife blade, and then peel it off. As for the marking left by the paper tape on the new flange, which may be rather sticky at this stage, cut round the flange edge with a coping saw to remove all the waste edge and to trim the flange to a neat parallel line at least 2" wide but not wider than 3". You will note that a rib to improve the register of the moulds has not been incorporated. This is because amateur moulds are not cleaned as carefully as one might wish, and register ribs do require a great deal of careful cleaning. This system using trapped nuts, bolts and flat flanges is quite satisfactory.

Chapter 6

Cockpits

When building a new boat, whether it be an adjustment of an existing boat or a completely new boat, you are faced with the necessity of putting the seat in the right place. Over the last ten years seat arrangements have developed from a shaped pan stuck to the floor (which always broke out), through a similar pan with canvas seat side or hip location pieces laced between seat edge and cockpit rim, to the first suspended seats which were deep, flat-bottomed, and right at the back of the cockpit rim so that on a reverse loop in surf one's kidneys received frightful blows from the back of the cockpit rim. Seat sides were made very wide for strength, and one's thighs suffered abrasions and contusions from the edges which bit deeply and cruelly into the legs. There has been a great deal of experimentation in seats and cockpits, and the present slalom-type cockpit with suspended seat is what most people will find themselves in, although the racing and sprint people have different methods.

It follows, therefore, that to make a new seat and cockpit from scratch is to attempt to gild the lily, and without previous knowledge one is highly likely to fail. So take a cockpit rim which suits the purpose, and a seat, maybe from another boat altogether, and adjust them, thereby making a new seat mould which will suit the new boat, and which may, just may, be an improvement on earlier cockpits. You can start from plaster casts and heated sheets of perspex laid over a tractor seat on to

138

which a willing patient sits, swathed in blankets to reduce the agony of a scorched sit-upon. Use this method if you will, but that was all done ten years ago.

It is almost always the case in new boats that the seat requires adjustment from a previous design. The new boat may require a seat more in the middle of the cockpit in line with current practice, or a seat which is higher up or lower down to suit the new hull depth or purpose of the boat. For example, a white-water slalom boat requires a low seat for stability, while a fast flat-water design requires a high seat so that the paddler can sacrifice stability for power on the water.

Assuming that you have the deck section, that the cockpit hole is right for the new boat, that the new deck section has been moulded into the new plug, and that the new moulds have been made and a new boat cast, one can then develop the seat.

Make a cockpit rim from the old moulds, with about 2″ of seat flange attached. This rim is then glassed into the new boat in the usual way. One then selects the seat pan required—it may be from the same mould that one took the cockpit rim, or it may be from some other mould altogether. Cast the seat in the usual way, and take it up to the cockpit rim but not beyond. Trim this to a clean edge so that it will fit behind the side flanges on the rim. Note that some seats will be wider than the cockpit rim to which they are to be fitted, so these will fit behind the rim flange. Others will be narrower, and these will fit on top of the rim flange.

Place the seat pan in position, and clamp it with four 'G' clamps, two each side, and play around with the seat pan until it seems right for longitudinal adjustment, is centrally placed laterally, is the right height, is not twisted nor tilted sideways, and has just about the right endways tilt on the seat. Three of these measurements are clearly neutral, but three are adjustable. When satisfied with the positioning, drill through the flanges, and countersink bolts on each side. Jam polystyrene blocks each side of the seat flanges between the seat and the inside of the hull, to stop seat sway (page 90).

The new canoe is then put to use for several weeks, and if necessary returned to the workshop for seat adjustment and re-positioning of the bolts holding the seat. Drill as many holes as

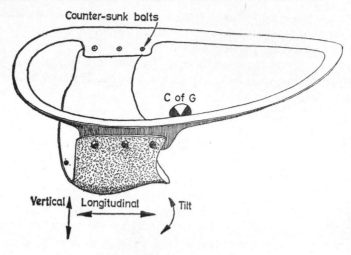

Counter-sunk bolts

C of G

Vertical Longitudinal Tilt

Making a new cockpit

you need, as position is important and holes can be filled.

When everyone is satisfied with the seat position, clean out the seat area, take out the polystyrene blocks, and tighten up the bolts. Roughen up the area round the seat flanges so that filler will stick, and use filler to obtain a smooth profile. Do not be afraid of a slightly bottle-shaped seat mould, as the mould can usually be popped off by using rotation and endways play. Make the seat area smooth with filler, and sand it to a coarse but smooth profile. There is no need to polish at this stage. Line the cockpit area with polythene sheet and polish the seat once, use release agent, and cast the cockpit mould *in situ*. Trim it when it is green (it is most important to clean up the edge easily), and leave it for a day.

Now try to release the seat, and you will find it very difficult. Some commercial people drill a tiny hole, $\frac{1}{16}''$ say, through the new mould but not through the seat, and use an airline to blow the seat mould out of the new cockpit. If you lack this facility, ensure that the cockpit rim is really clean, back to the original cockpit rim, with no gelcoat or lap-over of resin or glass from the new mould on to the seat and cockpit edges. The slightest keying of the mould to the cockpit will cause a very strong

140

bond which resists the efforts to separate one from the other.

Eventually you will be able to lift the fore edge of the cockpit rim mould up a little, and the back edge. Using a rubber pad and a mallet, again with great care (not a job for enthusiastic youth), thump the inside of the seat mould all over until it separates. Use a bricklayer's bolster to ease up the side of the cockpit rim and quite suddenly it will pop up and come out.

This first mould will be quite rough, so trim the edges quite cleanly, taking care not to cut back so much that the rim becomes inadequate for holding the spray deck, and then start the rubbing-down procedure, 180 grade wet and dry, 360, 600, followed by a thorough buffing with the drill mop and medium and fine cutting paste. Finally run-in the seat mould as for the hull and deck moulds.

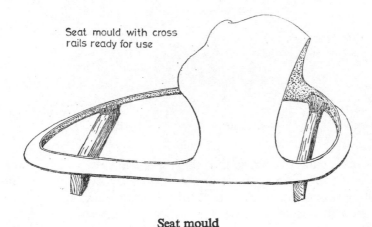

Seat mould with cross rails ready for use

Seat mould

The new cockpit mould is not yet ready for taking off casts. In order to work easily on the new cockpit mould, glass two rails across on to the rim of the mould, so that the mould will sit level on a bench top without rocking about. Two or three layers of mat and resin are enough to fix the rails to the mould as shown. Make sure that the rails are fixed parallel without any twist on them, otherwise it will be necessary to plane one rail until it is parallel with the other.

141

As a variation on this method, use a plywood plate across the mould between the seat flanges, with a hole cut centrally, large enough to accept a 2″ diameter alloy tube. Using the TV aerial fittings one can get with old alloy poles from the scrapyard, clamp a short length of pole to the bench edge, and drop

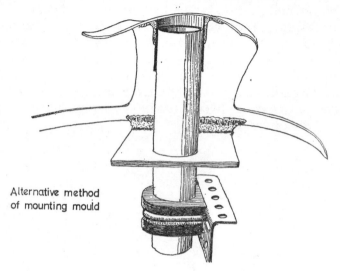

Alternative method of mounting mould

Alternative seat mould mounting

the seat mould over it, so that the upper end engages in a socket glassed to the seat pan. It is now possible to turn the mould round as one works on it, and this saves time and mess.

As a matter of interest the seat mould shown is typical of those in use two or three years ago, with the seat pan rather too close to the back rim for comfort in extreme use where Steyr lay-back rolls are necessary. Some seats will have thigh braces built into them, but these are uncommon and sometimes a problem for novices who do not wish to be locked into the cockpit.

The 'jelly mould' seat mould
The type of cockpit or seat mould illustrated is recent in development. There is only one firm at present using this type of

'Jelly mould' seat mould

mould, but they are hired out so that many amateur builders are likely to use one in the next few years.

The firm is more used to pattern making and high-quality mouldings for marine purposes than to canoeing moulds, and they have brought pattern-making practice into canoe mould design. This type has an advantage in that the wet laminates can be rolled right up to the edge, and when the cast has hardened and lifted off the mould it has a clean edge when trimmed with a coping saw. It is not possible to trim this type of cast when it is wet, but as trimming when hard takes only a few minutes extra and the quality of the finished job is almost always better, especially for the amateur, it is worth it. On the illustration the plain area shows where the seat cast goes. Having an area beyond that on to which one can go is an advantage.

Cockpit 'pod'

One aim of every canoe designer is to make the canoe as unsinkable as possible. The principles involved in this idea are not new, but really it is a 'try-on' to put what is design, as yet unproved, into a construction book, so approach this with caution. Certain principles are involved, though, which may help you to build a better boat.

143

The sketch H shows how it should work. The paddler sits in a slot in the canoe deck, and when the canoe is laid over there is sufficient buoyancy in the sides of the canoe to keep the cockpit edge above water; if below water, the slope of the pod sides will keep the water back. When the canoe comes upright, the

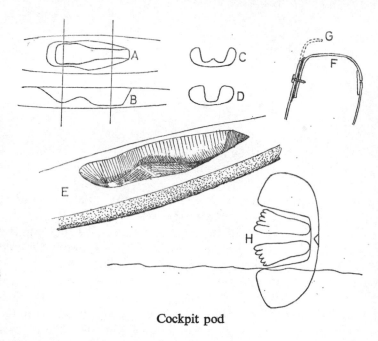

Cockpit pod

water along the edge should mostly drain outside the canoe, and that inside should be a minimum. Where the knees go will need to be a bit wider, so some draining point will be required here. In use, upright, the canoe may take on water by splashing, but laying the boat right over should tip the water out. The thoughtful reader will realise that this is going to involve wet canoeing, and so it will. However, this is for fun canoeing, such as surfing and polo and just playing about. Think: no spray deck, no fear of being trapped as a beginner, it's as easy as falling off a log. The trouble will be to stay in, but we are working on that.

Sketches A, B, C, and D, are self-explanatory giving plan,

profile, and two sections as shown. E is the general appearance. Sketch F shows that the hull and deck are joined in the usual way, but the pod is fitted to the inside of the curl down of the deck, having about a 2″ overlap all round. The pod is fitted dry at first, and self-tapping screws fitted to hold it exactly in place. The screws are removed and the two mating surfaces are roughened, given a thick coat of gelcoat and fitted together again then the screws put in. When the gelcoat has set the screws are removed, but the short experience we have had so far shows that the gelcoat tends to crack loose. Replacing the self-tapping screws with pop rivets would clearly help, as then the mechanical strains involved would be taken by these and the resin would merely seal the pod into the deck.

The dotted outline 'G' shows that a curled rim could easily be fitted to the rim of the pod, using the same sealing method, and this would permit a large spray deck to be fitted thus making all-weather dry canoeing possible. One would need to take care not to trip over the spray deck when rushing to the water, new canoe on shoulder.

The whole canoe is sealed off, and so provides maximum possible buoyancy. In the event of a capsize, one simply tilts the canoe on its side and it is self-draining. There cannot be any fatalities of the trapped feet variety. The sealed hull will almost certainly take in water, so a large drain hole must be fitted. It is clear that in surfing, sudden compressions on the hull would tend to fire the stopper out with explosive violence, and so this must be placed not to strike passing bathers. A length of string might limit its range. In addition, the hull must have a form of buoyancy, of the solid foam type fitted—a block between rear deck and hull would be suitable, otherwise in case of complete swamping the dense grp material would sink.

We tried one idea where the legs were placed slightly apart with an 'island' of deck between. This failed because the edge of the pod was below water level when at 90°, and we could see that a young lad could do himself a mischief if the canoe stopped suddenly.

This item must come last in this chapter. It has not yet been proved to be 'the' answer, but like most things in boats, it could be 'an' answer to some problems. The lads in the club are not

K

head over heels in love with the idea yet, and it is an odd experience to sit on a canoe rather than in it, and one's knees look so vulnerable stuck up in the air. The thing has been rolled in the rough in a weir, with the aid of a quick-release strap right round the hull and deck and thighs, but when the paddler got to the bank to get out, he could not release the quick-release buckle as it had jammed. We are not using belts at the moment as it could be too dangerous.

Chapter 7

Rudders and skegs

Rudder types

There are many different ways of applying steadying or turning power to a canoe. Each hull will have certain characteristics: some will pivot around a point which is central, under the paddler, some will pivot around a point just in front of the paddler, and some will pivot about a point just behind the paddler. The most usual is the stern-turning boat which pivots around a point just in front of the paddler, probably under his knees.

For some uses, the canoe must turn easily and without hindrance and with the minimum amount of equipment, i.e. the slalom canoe plus paddle. In some cases needs must dictate that a turning hull must be used for unsuitable purposes, e.g. a long river or sea trip. In that case the hull must be stiffened in the water, and given directional stability. This is done by attaching a fixed rudder or skeg.

Some canoes are naturally stiff in the water, such as a racing K1, the hull being long and narrow with little rocker, and it is slow to turn. Turning this is done most efficiently by having an under-hull rudder about 2 ft forward of the rearmost end of the boat. This has drawbacks. In rough water a rudder blade toward the end of the canoe may often be out of the water, especially with a following wave system. The under-hull rudder will be wiped off if one tries to shoot a shallow weir, and so a

147

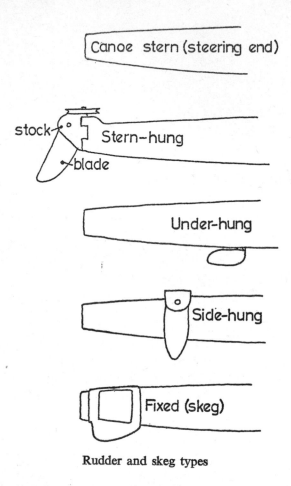

Canoe stern (steering end)

stock — Stern-hung
— blade

Under-hung

Side-hung

Fixed (skeg)

Rudder and skeg types

time-consuming portage is necessary. While the other competitor with a stern-hung rudder will be shooting the weir and making up time.

Another approach which has never been properly tried is the side-hung rudder, after the method of steering Viking ships. In this the rudder blade can knock-up both backwards and forwards, whereas the stern-hung rudder may only knock-up backwards.

If you study the effect of applying, say, right rudder to avoid an obstacle on the left of the bows, the theory of couples will prove that with a stern rudder of any kind, the steering effect will be to initiate a turning movement towards the right, but there will be a slight acceleration of the centre of gravity of the whole towards the left, that is towards the obstacle. Now, to avoid the sideways component towards trouble, if one applies the turning effort towards the bows, the couple effect will initiate the necessary turning effect, but the centre of gravity of the whole will be accelerated away from the obstacle, i.e. towards the right. That is why a slalomist knows that a high telemark is more effective than a low telemark when avoiding obstacles, because the high telemark provides a pull towards the centre of the turn, whereas the low telemark provides a 'hanging-out' of the stern away from the centre of the turn. Theory shows that bow-hung rudders should be more effective, but no one ever uses them.

In general rudders are a complication, and are easily damaged. A good paddling action usually gets over most problems, and if one is driven to it, a skeg will help beginners with directional instability or deep-sea paddlers who need a rest from constant steering effort in side winds. The racing paddler must of course have a rudder in order to generate maximum paddling effort. It is interesting to note that Canadian-style racing demands that no rudder be fitted, this being part of the class regulations.

Stern-hung rudder assembly
The parts are lettered. The construction uses alloy sheet.
A   The fin may be riveted or bolted to the stern of the boat.
B   The steering wires are given a complete turn round the pulley and clamped by the bolt, C.
C   Cable clamping bolt, Bowden cable.
D   The rudder pivot. The curved end engages in hole in bracket, E.
E   The rudder pivot anchor.
F   The rudder stock cheeks, riveted to spacer.
G   The stock spacer, slightly thicker than the rudder blade. The same material is used in the fin spacer.
H   The blade. That shown is for clear, deep water. Weedy water will pile up rubbish around a straight blade, so an

angled leading edge is necessary in weedy waters. The angle should be not less than 45° to the vertical.

The ideal blade has an aspect ratio in profile of 1 : 5. The ideal cross-section is streamlined, aspect ratio 1 : 20. The profile shape should be parabolic, or nearly so.

If the blade is made to enter 7″ into the water, this gives a

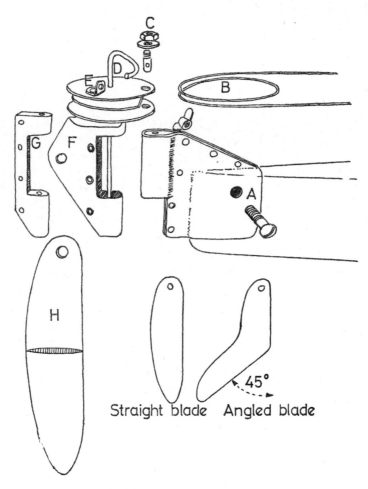

Straight blade   Angled blade

Rudder assembly, stern hung

blade width of 1·4″. This gives a blade thickness of ·07″, that is about $\frac{1}{16}$″. Alloy bends too easily, so stainless steel is better.

The pivot of the blade should be large in diameter, say $\frac{1}{2}$″ at least. No sizes are given as each will vary with the boat and the purpose, but try not to put anything under the waterline that has nothing to do with turning. In other words, only the rudder blade should be in the water.

Several points to note when making rudders follow.

1 A useful cable clamp is made from the brass terminal blocks which are found in the plastic terminal clusters one can buy at Woolworth's.

2 Another cable anchor to fix the cable to the frying pan, or the rudder stock, is the Bowden cable-clamping bolt which is found on bicycle brakes. A simple clamp can be made by taking an ordinary brass bolt, $\frac{3}{16}$″ say, and drilling a hole through the shaft of the bolt just under the head. The hole will be $\frac{1}{16}$″.

3 A knock-up blade is fine, as it simply knocks out of the way if it strikes an obstacle. One may rely on the weight of the blade to bring it back down into use again, which demands a friction-free action and a blade heavy enough to stay down against the pressure of the water. An elastic return can be devised.

4 In competition, at the start, a dirty trick sometimes encountered is the gentle bending of an opponent's rudder blade, so that it is up and stays up, or the slackening of his cable clamps. Wise racing paddlers should wrap the clamps in tape, and make the rudder blades strong enough to resist bending.

5 The cable used for controlling the rudder should be Bowden cable enclosed in a plastic sheath. Unsheathed cable will rust very easily.

6 Cable guides can be made from $\frac{1}{8}$″ polythene tubing.

Rudder controls

If one has a movable rudder, there must be some way to move it. The most popular method of steering with the under-hung rudder is to use the kick-stick. In the racing craft the feet are

151

'pedalling' in the racing drive, and so if the tiller bar method were to be used, the feet would constantly be wagging the rudder in the water thus causing drag. In touring boats this foot action is not so evident, and so a tiller bar is not ruled out.

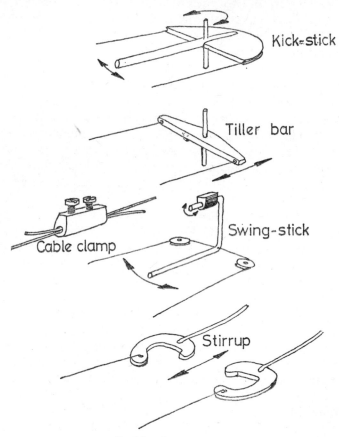

Kick-stick

Tiller bar

Cable clamp

Swing-stick

Stirrup

Rudder foot controls

The kick-stick (see also pp 153-55) lies horizontally between the feet, and a touch inwards with one foot or the other causes the stick to be kicked to one side or the other, and to turn the 'frying-pan' half pulley on the vertical central pivot, thus pulling the rudder wires one way or the other. The frying-pan pulley is made rather more than exactly a half circle so that the wire is always coming away at a tangent to the rim of the frying pan. If, as in the tiller bar, the wire comes away at the end of the bar, there is a slackening of the wire at any point but dead centre, and so the rudder usually feels sloppy and lacks definition which is unacceptable for most skilful paddlers.

The stirrup system is one I used long ago in a sailing canoe, a very ordinary touring boat, and it worked very well. The wires are attached to plywood stirrups like the letter 'G' and they are hung on to the internal framework of the canoe with powerful elastic. I used $\frac{1}{4}''$ catapult elastic. The wires are always in tension, it is easy to fit, and there are no spindles to wear out or jam. However, the notion of baling out of a tight cockpit with twanging elastics and springy wires flopping about is quite frightening. Perhaps a simple, foolproof system could be devised on this basis. It is sensitive to foot pressures, so it would be unsuitable for racing craft or racing paddling styles.

One method which I have never seen used is the swing stick method, where the bar hangs down from a high longitudinal pivot. This needs pulleys however, or guide tubes, to turn the wire.

A method, not shown, is based on the sculling boat, the 'tooth-pick'. In this the sculler sets his feet into leather 'shoes' on the footplate, so that he can come forward on his sliding seat using the thigh muscles, ready for the drive. The right foot (or left) is on an alloy plate with turned-up edges, which pivots at floor level. By turning his toes inwards or outwards the sculler can operate a rudder wire, thus operating an under-hull rudder.

KICK-STICK ASSEMBLY. The 'frying-pan' is made from alloy sheet and rivets. The stick is alloy tube, as is the spindle. The top and bottom spindle blocks are wood or resin blocks. The parts are as follows:

A   The stick. Alloy tube or paddle shaft material will do. It is flattened and riveted to the pan.

B   The 'frying-pan' is made from three sheets of alloy, riveted together and to the tube. The space between the top and

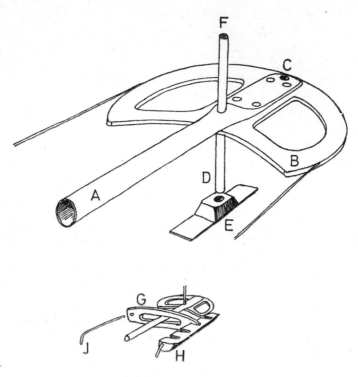

Kick-stick assembly

bottom sheets of the pan must be slightly thicker than the thickness of the wire to be used.

C   The hole for the wire anchor bolt.
D   The vertical spindle; a hollow alloy tube will do.
E   The bottom block. This could be alloy, riveted to a base plate which in turn is glassed to the bottom of the boat, or it could be of wood, drilled and glued to the frame of the boat, if wood.
F   Where the top block goes. This can be a simple block, and the natural flexibility of the hull and deck will allow the spindle to be entered. Alternatively a block can be bolted to the framework after the lower end of the spindle has been put into its hole. It is possible simply to drill a hole

in the deck and to push a pivot rod down to engage in the open top end of the pivot tube.

G   This drawing shows the footrest arrangement. This is the plate for the feet through which the kick stick passes.

H   The side block attached to the hull which takes the foot-rest plate in slots.

J   The footrest plate is held in the slots by long pins.

Skegs

This part of the book was completed, until I met Mick Powell of Worcester at a conference of amateur canoe builders which is held each autumn at Wollaston near Wellingborough. His idea is so simple, so light when made, and so easy to make, that it must be written up and replace the older, more tedious method.

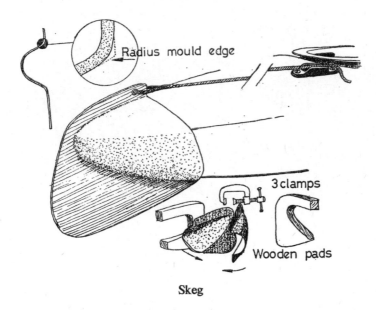

Skeg

The outline drawing shows the general appearance of the skeg which fits over the extreme end of the kayak. The smaller drawing shows how the two casts are fitted together.

A longer or deeper or larger skeg is needed on the sea, or

when someone light is using the boat, as rough water often cocks the end up so that the skeg becomes ineffective, and a light person loads the kayak so little that it rides high in the water, so the skeg does not reach right into the water. Experience will tell you which skeg size will suit your needs. One all-embracing idea is simply to cast a flange on to the skeg, top and bottom much the same, and then bolt varying skeg sizes on to that flange.

MAKING THE MOULD. Cut a sheet of alloy or Formica-faced wood to the shape of the largest skeg required. Allowance must be made for the topside flange as well, through which the attachment hole will be drilled. The end of the kayak is polished and given a coat of release agent. The shaped plate is offered up, and cut until it fits neatly to the profile of the kayak. Care must be taken to line it up along the centre line.

Fix the plate in place with masking tape, or blobs of Plasticine, so that one half can be gelcoated and laminated easily. The laminate should extend forward about 8″ to 10″ from the extreme end of the kayak. Leave to set. Remove the plate, and polish and release the other side of the kayak and the new skeg-shaped flange. Gelcoat and cast in the usual way. Two laminates of 1½-oz mat should be quite enough. Leave to set. Drill one hole straight through where the attachment cord will eventually go. Release from the kayak and clean up the two half moulds. Ensure that the two parts are shaped as one, so that the register on the hull will be accurate in due course. This is now the mould.

CONSTRUCTION. Polish and release the moulds. Use gelcoat if you wish to make a good job of it, but this is not essential. Laminate one layer of 1½-oz mat on to each of the moulds straightaway, one after the other. Roll well, and while they are wet, clamp them together firmly so that the wet inner faces of the skeg flange will bind and set together. The clamping load must be spread by wooden pads, otherwise the resin will be squeezed out under the clamp pressure. When it is hard, remove the moulds, and then clean up the light thin skeg shell; drill the hole for the attachment cord, and attach the skeg to the stern of the kayak with cord to a clam cleat just behind the cockpit, or by a short elastic to the toggle on the deck.

The inner surface of the skeg will be rough, the outer surface highly polished. One—or two—colour skegs can be made. The moulds can turn out one skeg in 20 minutes if heat is used. Cost, a few pence.

Chapter 8

Accessories

Make your own helmet

First of all, don't. Don't make it as a substitute for a motor-cycle helmet, because it will not do. This helmet is designed for low velocity impact. It won't do for rock climbing, because falling sharp-edged pebbles will go through the slots cut in the shell in order to spill water. You could make it without slots, and then possibly it would do for rock climbing, but check with a rock-climber first. Without slots, the helmet contains water, and rolling is made more difficult, just at a time when it is important not to have extra difficulties.

You need a mould, and some knowledge of what is required.

A   The shell, made of two laminations of 1½-oz mat. Some use one lamination of 1½-oz mat and one lamination of 10-oz cloth.

B   The liner is available from Pyrene-Panorama Ltd, Hanworth Air Park, Feltham, Middlesex. It is riveted into the shell. Make sure that the final angle of the shell on the head is correctly adjusted.

C   The holes cut to allow water out. A tank cutter on a drill bit will do very well.

D   Rivet heads.

E   Pieces of heavy plastic sheet, with slots cut to take the chin strap, and riveted to the helmet shell.

F   A rubber rim, especially important around the front. It is made of neoprene rubber strip, such as is used in wet suit

158

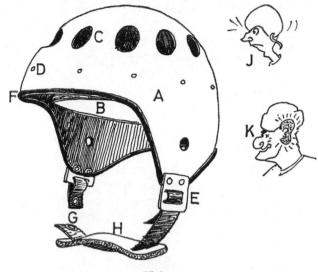

Helmet

seam reinforcement, and glued on.

G   Popper press-stud fasteners.

H   Chin pad of 4-mm neoprene foam wet suit material.

J   A chap who failed to fasten the strap on this type of helmet, and collected a badly bruised nose. It happened.

K   A canoe polo player of the old school, using a commercial helmet as supplied to ice hockey players, which regrettably exposes the ears to impact from passing paddle blades. If you would like to enhance your rugged good looks by sporting a couple of cauliflower ears, then do use one of these helmets and play polo. On the other hand, these helmets are not expensive, costing about the same as a cheap paddle, they float, look good, and are quite good for ordinary use.

Remember, it's your head, your life maybe. In this department it's better to buy than to bodge.

Make your own spray deck

First of all, don't. Not if you wish to avoid one possibility of being trapped in a canoe. If the seal around the waist is good,

159

if the seal around the cockpit rim is good, and if you cannot break that seal, then any attempt to get out of the canoe simply results in a pressure difference effect which holds the body in the canoe. Trying to withdraw the lower part of the body from the canoe, with the seam complete, is like trying to withdraw the handle of a bicycle pump, where the washer won't allow air to pass it, and your finger is over the connection end. There is suction inside the canoe, and pressure outside. A pressure difference of $\frac{1}{4}$ lb per square inch, spread over 300 square inches of spray deck area, is 75 lbs thrust holding you in.

However, any reasonably advanced canoeing requires a spray deck as an essential part of it, and there are ways of dealing with the problems of breaking the seal around the cockpit rim.

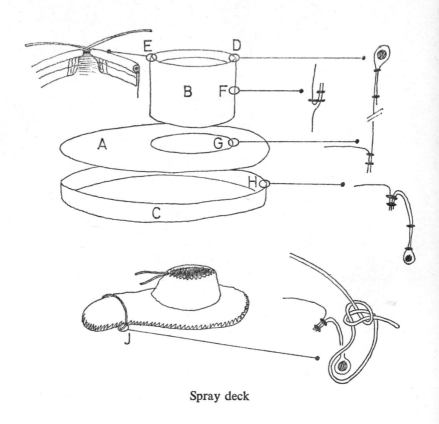

Spray deck

You can make your own spray deck for about £1.25 and the drawing shows the essential parts, but you can buy quite a good commercial one for only just over twice that cost.

A   Lay brown paper over the cockpit hole, and trace the outline of the cockpit rim edge on to the paper. Now draw around that a further ½″ beyond. Cut the material to that pattern. The hole in the middle must be big enough for the hips to pass through, and the centre of the hole is just over the front centre of the seat.

B   A cylinder of material, with a perimeter 2″ more than the perimeter of the hole in A. The depth is 12″.

C   The cockpit rim seal. The perimeter is the outer perimeter of A plus 2″, and the depth is 4″.

D   The top edge of the body cuff. Lay in a long piece of cord, fold over about 1½″ of material, and either pin or staple the material over until the first line of stitching is put in, about 1″ below the fold. The ends of the cord remain outside the cuff at the ends.

E   The front end of the cuff, top edge, where the open ends of the material are turned under and stitched back on the inside of the cuff. The cord is left for a tie to be made. A de-luxe system would be to tie a length of elastic to the cord end, and then another length of cord to the end of the elastic, so that the whole assembly could be pulled through. The elastic would be about half the perimeter of the top edge of the cuff. A non-slip knot is necessary then, between cord and elastic, for if they should separate, it is a difficult job to get the cord through again. After the tie is established the second line of stitching goes in, as close to the elastic as possible.

F   The vertical seam on the cuff. The two edges are seamed face to face, then turned over and the whole stitched right through to lock the seam. This seam could be fore or aft of the cuff. If fore, it would help to make the tie opening at E.

G   The cuff is stitched into the spray deck, ends turned in, double stitched.

H   The seam between the rim cuff and the deck is made with a long piece of cord already in place in the turn-over. The two edges of the cuff are pinned or stapled to the edge of the deck, and stitched right around. The cord ends are left hanging out at the end of the cuff. The cuff is stitched again about an inch from the turn-over, all round. The seam to the deck edge is double stitched. The cord is then tied to the end of the elastic, and the whole pulled through. The length of the elastic can be varied, depending on its thickness and the required tension in the cuff. $\frac{3}{16}''$ square aero or catapult elastic from a model shop does quite well, and something like $\frac{5}{6}$ the perimeter of the cuff is about right for the length of the elastic. The knot is a sheet bend with wire tightly wrapped around the knot, especially the ends. When the elastic is in place, the cuff should again be stitched close to the elastic. If not, the canoeist will have difficulty adjusting the spray deck in use.

J The spray deck must have a release strap, or panic strap. When you need it, you know you are about to drown, so your movements tend to be powerful and quick. A piece of webbing is all right, but the stitching rots so that when you need it you pull like mad and the strap comes loose. Better to tie a cord around the elastic, which means piercing the spray deck material through the cuff. Tie the knot as a bowline. Allow sufficient length in the cord to allow the spray deck to fit properly on to the cockpit rim.

The material used is usually proofed nylon, but a superior specialist spray deck can be made from 3-mm foam neoprene as used for wet suits. It should not be so thick that it would not go on or stay on the cockpit rim.

Carrying canoes on roof racks

The average canoe receives as much damage being carried about as being used. The scuffing of the highly polished surface is usual when canoes are lashed to the cross bars on a roof rack. Wind pressures when travelling at speed cause the boat to veer about on the roof, and this causes scuffing between the rails and the canoe.

Most rough-water canoeists find that after a few weeks of regular use their canoe is so battered anyway that any attempt at guarding against scuffing is a waste of effort. However, there are many people with high quality boats, both in veneer and glass, which are kept looking well and should be guarded against scuffing.

METHOD. Lay the canoe on the roof rack, and mark where the cross rails are in relation to the deck ridge. Polish the deck ridge, using release agent, and cast a pad, 3-oz lay-up, about 8″ long at this point (use masking sheets around the area of work to guard against resin splashes on the rest of the boat). When this deck pad is hard, release it and clean up the boat and cut and file the pad to a neat profile.

Canoe deck

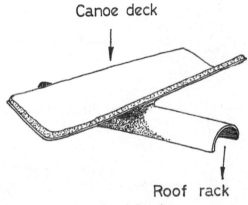

Roof rack

Roof rack bracket

Drape a double thickness of pre-wetted glass and resin over the polished cross-rail, and let it hang there until hard. It should be about 6″ long. Remove it, and clean up. Use polythene to guard the car roof against resin drips.

The two pieces are now laid across each other at right angles, and some way to clamp them together while they are stuck with resin dough is found. Two longer pieces of wood, clamped at their ends, one along the 'V' of the deck pad and one under the half-round rail piece, will do very well. Mix up a very small quantity of catalysed gelcoat and glass mat scraps, and make a dough which is formed around the crossing of the pad and the rail piece with the fingers. Leave this to harden, remove clamps, and clean up finally. Take a piece of neoprene wet suit material and glue this on to the deck pad.

163

Canoe Building

One pad is required for the fore deck and one aft. The pads are self-adjusting. The canoe is placed upside down on the pads with the deck ridge on the 'V' of the pad, and lashed firmly down. The pads could be lost if the canoe jolts loose through the lashings coming undone, so a short length of cord to tie the pads to the cross rails is a useful safety device. Alternatively they can be fastened there permanently.

The pads are small, neat and effective. My thanks to Mick Powell of Worcester for this idea.

Make your own car roof rack in grp
This is the type of rack which I have used in the five and a half years I have had the car, and at various times it has carried six baths canoes, three slalom kayaks and an upturned Irish curragh all the way back from Galway Bay to Oxford. That weighed well over 200 lbs. It works, it is inexpensive, and it protects the car roof. It even improves soundproofing and heat insulation, too. It takes about ten hours to make.

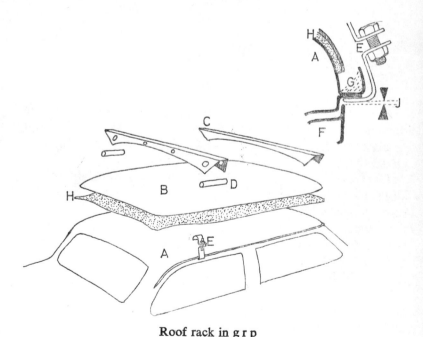

Roof rack in g r p

1   Polish the car roof (A) with mould release wax, and mask all round the roof gutter edge. If the gutter is narrower across its open top edge than its bottom, the resin drips will fill it up, and form a solid dovetail which will have to be torn out. So fill the gutter first with a wedge of wax or Plasticine (G).

2   Cover the whole car with papers, as the resin does splash some distance from the job. Use release agent all over the area to be covered. Lay on a layer of gelcoat when the release agent is dry. About 2 lbs is enough for a 1500 cc saloon car roof. When this has set, use two layers of $1\frac{1}{2}$-oz mat, and laminate this in the usual way.

3   When this cast is set hard after 24 hours (the car can be driven as soon as the resin is green), pull it off the roof, and trim the edges (B). The edge should clear the gutter bottom, or corrosion and inadequate draining of the car roof will result.

4   Next, obtain a piece of foam plastic sheet (H), about $\frac{1}{4}''$ thick, and lay it on the roof of the car. Lay the cast over it and trim to shape. Cut pieces of cardboard to the shape shown at (C). These make the cross-member bearers. Obtain four roof-rack clamps from Halfords, or make them (E). These lock on to a piece of alloy tube (D) at each corner—a piece of old tent pole or TV aerial tube will do. Tube is better than rod, as the lashings for the canoes pass through it.

5   Before glassing over the two cross-members, they must be placed on the roof, preferably as far apart as possible, but not more than 6 ft apart. Their positions will decide where the clamps are to fit, so the cross-members must not be placed so that the clamps are away from the gutter edge. Note also that many car roofs have little clearance between the bottom of the gutter (G) and the top of the car door (F) so it is essential to ensure that a sufficient clearance (J) is available when the clamp is in place.

6   When satisfied with the placing of the cross-members, tape the cardboard formers (C) into place, and put the job into the workshop. However, it may be better to leave it on the car roof, as any flexing or distortion in the roof rack (B) whilst the cross-members are setting will be permanent.

7   Glass the cardboard on with two layers of $1\frac{1}{2}$-oz mat. When these are hard, stand the rack on edge, and trim the ends of the

165

cross-members to size. Then using two layers of pre-wetted glass, form a patch into the open ends of the cross-members, to allow room to fit the alloy tube (D) on the open side of the closure. When the four patches have been made, allow them to harden then trim to a neat edge.

8   Put the cast roof (B) back on to the car roof, and check it for fit, especially at the gutter edges. When satisfied, take it off and fit four more tubes through the bearers, with even spacing between. These can slip out, so it helps to cut a trough across the bearer where the tube is to go, and slot it in from above. Glass into place and poke the glass patches along inside the cross-member (C). Then cut a small piece of card to cover the slot thus left, and glass over that to blend in with the profile of the cross-member.

9   The tube (D) can be locked in place by flattening it slightly when it is in place, and by slightly belling the exposed ends.

This roof rack protects the car roof from damage and in the course of time the slight vibration between the car roof and the plastic sponge liner raises a brilliant polish on the roof. It does however, tend to encourage corrosion around the gutter edge. Mine was faulty through being too deep into the gutter. It is very firm and it has never shifted no matter what load has been put on it. One can even stand on it provided the weight is over the cross-members.

Make your own canoe trailer
The enthusiastic canoeist will usually find that the local waters are insufficient for his needs. If the water will not come to him then he and his canoes must go to the water. Certainly a reliable trailer is essential for any canoeing group, unless there are many car roofs available.

Certain basic measurements are required, and certain basic design factors must be considered. A drawing with measurements could be given, but a drawing with indications as to which measurements are necessary will be more flexible, and you must design your own trailer.

The drawing shows the required measurements, A to L.

A   The overall length of the longest canoe to be carried.

B   The distance between end supports, normally half of A

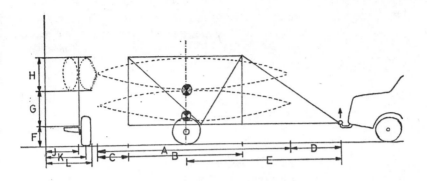

Canoe trailer measurements

but if really short canoes are to be carried as well, then it must be about 2 ft shorter than the overall length of the shortest canoe to be carried. This would be incompatible with carrying K2s and canoe polo boats.

C This overhang in Britain should not exceed $3\frac{1}{2}$ ft. Vehicle construction and use regulations are published by the Government and should be consulted first. Questions of abnormal loads come in when the rear overhang is excessive, and what is regarded as excessive is stated in regulations.

D The distance from the front of the longest canoe to the towing point, about 18″.

E Half A, plus D. The longer the towing arm, the steadier the tow will be, and the easier it will be to reverse the vehicle. I call long more than 12 ft, when the trailer is hitched to a 15-ft long car.

F This must allow sufficient ground clearance when going from a level surface to a steep slope, either up or down. The longer E is, the higher F must be made. If E is 12 ft, F is about right at 18″.

G The beam of the average canoe to be carried, so a 23.6″-beam slalom kayak would have a 24″ space here. However, the Mirror dinghy, very popular, will fit into a space 5 ft by 26″, so alternative uses of the trailer must be considered.

167

H   The same as G, unless some alternative use affects this. F, G and H, taken together, should be a few inches more than the height of the car roof, so that an exceptionally long load, such as a K4, can be carried without colliding with the car roof.

J   Half the width of the trailer between uprights. This should be some multiple of the depth of the canoes to be carried, usually 12″ each, so a 5 ft overall width, i.e. J equals 2½ ft, would be right.

K   Half the track of the trailer, and as wide as possible without causing the overall width of the vehicle to exceed 7 ft in Britain. Wider than that would introduce handling difficulties and possible conflict with the construction and use regulations. Garage opening must also be considered.

L   Half the overall width of the trailer. The middle and top rail are full width, the lowest rail is not more than twice J. An extra canoe can be fitted into the top slot, provided L less J is not less than 8″. The bottom slot is occupied by the wheel and it would be very unwise to try to fit a canoe here, even though when at rest it can be fitted in. On full rebound the wheel can rip through the canoe shell in a second or so.

LOADING. The centre of gravity of the load should be directly in line with the centre of gravity of the centre frame of the unloaded trailer. This in its turn should be directly over the point of contact of the wheel with the ground. The fore triangle of the trailer frame has its own weight, and this is carried partly by the wheels and partly by the towing hitch. The nose loading should be about 56 lbs whether the trailer is carrying a load or not.

LIGHTING. In Britain the trailer must carry rear red lights, rear red triangle towing sign, flashing indicators, brake light, number plate and light. If the trailer is wider than the towing vehicle by more than 11″ each side, then it must have forward-shining white lights too. No light should be more than 3½ ft above the ground.

BUILDING SEQUENCE:

1   Draw out the side frame shape on the workshop floor
2   Cut the steel, 2″ × 1″, 12-gauge rectangular steel tube

3   Fit the pieces to the chalked outline
4   Weld up two sides, identical in shape. Tacking only will do
5   Cut four full-width cross-members
6   Cut two cross-members, reduced width, for the bottom of
    the frame
7   Chalk a rectangle on floor, exact size, dead square at
    corners
8   Brace the side frames exactly upright, and clamp the first
    cross-member
9   Weld up the cross-frames, one at a time, checking square-
    ness
10 Turn upside down the centre frame thus made

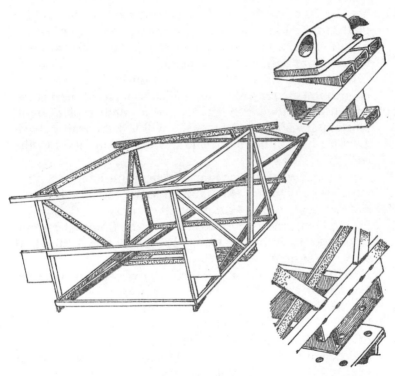

Canoe trailer frame

11 Chalk out long 'A'-frame pieces on the floor and cut the steel

12 Clamp these to the underneath side of the frame, now on top

13 Spot-weld in place, ensuring that the front ends are not less than 4" apart

14 Weld on spacer pieces where the axle cross-members must be attached

15 Cut, fit and weld the axle cross-members to the spacers and 'A'-frames

16 Cut, fit and weld two plates to the axle cross-members to provide base plates to which the suspension units are attached. Flexitor Number 6 units are about right, but it depends on total load

17 Set the framework upright on floor; cut, fit and weld a platform of short odd pieces of tubing to provide a platform for the towing hitch. This should be a 50-mm international size ball, with braking device

18 Cut, fit and weld number plates, ensuring they are large enough to take rear, stop and indicator lights at both sides, with triangle towing reflectors and a number plate light, plus numbers. If several vehicles will tow the trailer, have a simple bolt-on number plate which is easily fitted to the back plate

19 Cut, fit and weld corner braces in the top frame

20 Complete any tack welds, chip off scale, and wire brush

21 Put two coats of red lead paint all over

22 Fit the lights, running cables through the frames; fit grommets into their holes, using the international standard seven-pin system

23 Fit the suspension units, so that the wheels run parallel. Toe-in is not necessary with rubber suspension

24 Fit the brakes, and check that they work

25 Fit the wheels. Tyres should be at least six ply—we use Michelin ZX tubed tyres on Austin 1800 wheels and brakes and they seem likely to last forever. Economise on wheels and tyres, and you may suffer the consequences on some remote valley road, with midnight approaching and no garages for miles

26 Fit mudguards over the wheels. It is against the law not to, and muddy wet roads will provide a rooster tail of spray, through which overtaking motorists cannot see, from unguarded wheels. Total cost if you can do your own welding is about £100 (1972).

Chapter 9

Repairs

There are two types of repair, the emergency repair and the workshop repair. One is made on a wet boat and the other on a dry boat.

WET REPAIR

The boat has been holed on the water, and you are standing on a river bank, the canoe is soaking wet, and sticky tape will not stick to a wet, polished boat. Dry the boat off as well as you can, even using a bunch of grass. Finish off with a dry cloth, the dry parts of your shirt if necessary, and tape the damage so that the edges are held together and the water is kept out. A canoe can have the whole end, about a foot's length, ripped off, and yet with careful use of tape the end can be stuck on again. An emergency repair, for example at sea where one cannot leave the boat, may be possible by pushing a piece of sponge or any soft material into the hole from the inside. This supposes that the hole is near the cockpit and that the hole is not too large, and that one is carrying suitable soft material. I have never used this idea with grp material, but it was a useful emergency repair for canvas canoes some years ago.

RIVERBANK EMERGENCY REPAIR. One method is used by the slalom fraternity, for example when damage must be repaired, in time for the next run in 2 hours. The boat is badly damaged, and the camp site is not dry, and the boat is soaking wet. Mop out and wipe the boat as much as possible. Rub brush cleaner on to the boat around the damaged area, and set fire to it. I accept no responsibility for singed eyebrows and burned-out tents. It must of course be done with the greatest of care, but a thin skin of solvent on a boat does not burn for more than a few seconds. Do, please, if you value your skin, replace the cork on the solvent bottle, and take it at least 50 ft away, and put the solvent soaked rag in the river, temporarily.

The slight warmth does dry off the damaged area fairly well. Mix up laminating resin, and fix the patch as for a workshop repair. Then heat the patch either by two people holding the boat so that the patched area is about 6″ above a stove, or by setting fire to the patch. This burns with a thick black smoke, and can go on for some time, and it can ignite the boat and destroy the lot, so take care. However, as one is either on wet grass, or close to the river, simply wait about ten seconds until the smoke is well established and the fire shows signs of taking hold. Gently lower the blazing patch and canoe on to the grass and roll it gently to and fro to put out the flame. Leave for a few minutes, rub off the worst of the soot, and you should have a patch, hot and hard in less than five minutes. If you roll the patch too soon on the grass you could rub it off, if too late the canoe is a bonfire. This idea is very hazardous, and hardly ever used. In dry woodland or on dry grass, a heath fire could result.

DRY REPAIR
There are several ways of drying a boat. You can wait until it dries out in a dry workshop, or leave it in hot sunshine until the surface is dry, or scorch it over a cooking stove until hot and dry—*beware of fire*—or wipe it dry with a dry cloth, or use solvent to evaporate the dampness.

The dryness of the repair is either thorough, right through every fibre of the damaged area, or superficial only. Clearly the better repair is that which has complete dryness, and this requires usually a week in a dry workshop until the drying out has finished.

Method of repair
First have the boat drying out for a week in the workshop. Before leaving it to dry, use a sponge and mop out all water

inside the boat. The easiest way to do this is to tilt the boat on to one gunwale, and the natural curve of the gunwale will bring all the enclosed water to the area nearest to the cockpit opening, where it is easy to mop out. Tipping out is not enough. If the enclosed water is salt, then it is better to flush out with fresh water before mopping out.

Mark out all the damaged places using a felt-tipped pen. This helps one to assess the total damage. After a good weekend on the Teifi or a severe weir-bashing exercise on the Thames, there may be as many as six or eight patches needed.

Take a coarse disc in the sander, and rough up the surface of the boat where the patch is to go. Do not cut down into the glass reinforcement—a surface roughening is enough. Sometimes the edges of the damaged area are buckled because they interfere with each other. In that case cut out as little as possible in the actual cut or hole in order to get the edges to line up with each other. The repair is done on the outside of the boat. The roughening should extend about $1\frac{1}{2}''$ all around the actual damage. Any shiny area will certainly lose its patch in a few weeks of further use.

Several different ways of making the patch are now possible. One is the quick setting method. Cut a single patch out of $1\frac{1}{2}$-oz mat, and have it ready for the resin. Mix a small quantity of gelcoat resin with colour to match the boat, and add about twice the usual amount of catalyst. Stir well, and then apply gelcoat to the area where the patch is to go. Lay on the patch and quickly paint gelcoat all over it. At once turn it over and similarly 'paint' the other side of the patch. Make sure it is in place, and go make any other patches, one after the other, leaving no time between patches. It is necessary to be quick, as the resin will be set inside ten minutes. Go back to the first patch, and drag the brush firmly over the surface to fluff it up a little, but not so much that the patch is badly distorted. This will give a very fine surface to the patch. Now stipple the patch down and if necessary use a roller to consolidate the fibres and resin. Brush over lightly once more, and a very smooth patch results. Go and do the others, with all speed. If a patch has started to set before you can consolidate it, peel it off, clean the area with solvent, and remake the patch.

174

This method leaves an obvious patch on the outside of the boat which may be too disfiguring for your needs, but it gives quick, effective patches. Other methods exist if you have the time, and these are described in the following pages.

Internal patch
Clean up the hole externally as far as possible. Look inside. The inner surface of the boat may be quite dirty with sand and mud. This must be cleaned off, and a wire brush will do that well, but only within hand's reach of the cockpit. End holes are very difficult. Having cleared away all loose material, dead leaves, weed etc, mop the canoe out internally with brush cleaner on a cloth, either hand-held or tied to a stick. Scrub with the solvent-soaked cloth to clean the interior as thoroughly as possible. Three or four wipings may be necessary.

Prepare the patch required as before, and make up some gelcoat resin as before. Brush resin around the area to be patched internally, and then pre-wet the patch, both sides, quickly, and immediately drop it into place over the area to be patched. Sometimes one must use the extension brush as used for making the joint in a canoe. Pat it down with the brush, working it as much as possible without actually distorting the patch, to get the air out. Leave it to set. When it is hard, sand the outer damaged area with coarse sandpaper—hand-held is better. Keep the sanded area small. Cut out all loose fibres in the damaged area. Mix up a tiny quantity of gelcoat and dab it into place to cover all the sanded area. The use of masking tape around it gives a clean edge to the outer resin patch. Leave this to harden for a day, then cut it down with a body file and sand off. If there are any more depressions in the surface, fill them up again with resin. Eventually you will get a smooth sanded surface which can then be brought up to a good polish with wet and dry glass paper, 180 grit, 360, then 600, and then cutting paste on a polishing mop, followed by mould wax polish.

Resin patch
Sometimes fibrous reinforcement is not necessary, as in a surf board. The repair method is to clean out the damage, cut out an insert block of foam material, and fit it into the damaged

175

area, then glass it in with one layer of 10-oz woven rovings. The surface is rough. Make a crater to surround the damaged area, using Plasticine. Tilt the boat so that the crater will not spill. Mix up some laminating resin, and pour a tiny quantity over the damage to cover the whole area. Vibrate the boat by tapping it, or by holding a rubber pad against it and applying an orbital sander, edge on, to the pad. This vibrates the tiny air bubbles out of the resin. Leave to set, remove the Plasticine, and file to required shape and polish.

Smooth-surfaced patch, external
The damaged area is prepared as before by sanding. A piece of alloy sheet is polished, and made ready to cover the damage. It may be that a piece of the boat is completely missing, perhaps as big as your hand. The alloy is shaped with care to cover the missing area. It is then taped lightly to the surrounding surface. Examine the fit of the plate from inside. The plate is removed, a patch is laminated on to the plate, and the plate replaced and taped firmly on to the boat. The boat is slung so that the plate is under the patch.

Smooth-surfaced patch, internal
The damaged area is cleaned up as before. Try to scratch the area surrounding the hole as little as possible. The alloy plate is taped to the outside of the hole as before, checked for fit, and removed. The inside of the boat around the hole is cleansed as for an internal patch. The plate is taped on again, and a pre-wetted patch is dropped into place internally. The patch is worked with the brush to ensure that it fits as closely as possible to the plate and to the edges. It is useful to make the patch double thickness, and to use lots of resin with it. Both these methods give a smooth-surfaced patch, but the internally applied patch is the better one.

Different patching systems
Mostly the methods described rely upon ordinary laminating of gelcoat resin. Alternatives exist.

There is a proprietary glazing tape called 'Sylglas' which is a putty-soaked tape, about 2" wide, protected by aluminium foil.

This will stick to wet surfaces, so it is not necessary to mop the surface dry first. It is rather sticky and messy but excellent for a quick repair where speed and convenience is dominant.

A German preparation, unobtainable in Great Britain, consists of a tin of what looks like gelcoat resin, into which is mixed very fine glass fibres. A catalyst is stirred in from a tube, and the mix sets in 10 minutes; no fibrous reinforcement is necessary, as it is already in the resin.

Holts motor car repair sets contain materials to make a repair, but the smallest kit costs about £1, and is clearly uneconomical; but if all else fails and cost becomes of secondary importance, buy a kit.

Isopon, David's P 38 filler, and similar two-part resin-based fillers of various kinds, can be used to smear into cracks, and even to stick glass cloth across a break. Bostik black outdoor adhesive, soluble in petrol or paraffin, is very good for sticky patches, but messy.

*   *   *

Loose cockpit
Some home-made canoes, and even some commercial canoes, suffer from loose cockpits from time to time. What usually happens is that the seat braces come loose, and seat sway is possible. This in turn levers away at the cockpit rim, and starts to tear the seat and to loosen the rim. First, always try to replace the loose cockpit and seat braces as soon as they come loose. Rip them out and make new ones.

You may find that despite early treatment, a part of the cockpit rim is clearly loose, but not free to come out. The damage is not serious. Using sandpaper, roughen around the deck edge just under the loosened cockpit rim, and the underneath of the rim. Carry the roughening about two inches beyond the apparent end of the loosening. Make narrow (1″) strips of glass mat and, using gelcoat resin, laminate these strips on the outside of the deck, and up and under the rim. This may affect the final cure.

M

If the cockpit has become very loose, then it must be removed completely, the whole area cleaned out thoroughly, and the cockpit put back into place as for a new boat, with new seat braces, of course.

Seat brace (quick method)

These do break out eventually, but they are quick to install. Clean the inside of the boat and the rough side of the seat around the hip flanges at the side. Ensure there is no water about. Cut four strips of 1½-oz glass mat, 2″ by 10″. Two are for one side, and two for the other. Pre-wet these with gelcoat resin, and laminate the two strips together on a wetting-out board. Lift them off with the fingers, and stand them at one side of the cockpit area to apply the seat brace to the other side. Fold the long strip and slip it forwards behind the seat side. Hold the front end of the bulging brace with one hand, and smooth the ends of the brace into place, one end to the inside of the hull, and the other end to the inside of the seat side. Laminating resin will not work as it is too wet and mobile, and the whole brace will slip out in a few moments, but gelcoat being sticky will stay in place. Leave the repair undisturbed for an hour, and then do not use the boat for another day, and the brace is good enough for a season at least. The brace should look like that in the illustration on canoe building (page 91).

Canoe surgery

A dramatic term; but some canoes can be rescued from ruin by bold treatment. It does happen that in a stopper on a weir or river, or in heavy surf, or on rocks on a rapid, a canoe can be smashed in half, or more usually, have one end sheared off. Very often one recovers most of the bits that are involved. The canoe is a write-off and worth nothing as it stands. However, by using about £2 worth of material, it can be rebuilt and sold for about £6 to £7 probably to a hard-up youngster. These rebuilds can serve very well. Certain methods are used, as follows:

WOVEN-ROVINGS JACKET. Assuming that the whole boat has been patched together, and any missing parts replaced, it may still be a floppy boat. Apply pressure with the thumbs on the curve where the bottom turns into the side, and it will bend inwards with little resistance where a good boat would be almost impossible to bend. The whole structure is riddled with stress cracks, and small delaminations, and so has gone 'floppy'. It is probably porous, too. The colour is poor, and the surface badly scored and scratched. Disc all over the hull to rough up the surface and to reduce big lumpy patches. Take out the end loops, and clean up to end including the trim stripe along the joint line and for half an inch beyond it up on to the deck.

Take a length of 10-oz woven rovings about half or even two-thirds, the length of the canoe, and drape it over the boat centrally. Use one edge of the woven material to follow the line of the gunwale on one side, and tape it lightly into place every 6″ with masking tape. Pull the cloth over the hull, and smooth it so that it takes up the curvature of the hull. The spare material will hang on the side away from the edge that has been taped into place. With a sharp knife, cutting on to the canoe, trim along and lay the spare material aside. Tape this cut edge to the boat with care. Mix up about 1½lbs of gelcoat, because it is more sticky when wet than laminating resin, and roll back one edge of the cut cloth to the centre line of the canoe, disturbing only one edge. Wet the hull with resin, then lay the cloth back in place. Ease it back into place thoroughly, and tape that edge again. Spare resin will cause the tape not to stick. When that edge is re-established, roll back the other edge, wet under it, re-lay, and tape down again. Now work more resin into the surface, and wet out thoroughly. Take up the spare glass which was trimmed off the central piece, and use this to cover the ends of the hull as before.

When the whole job has set, and is 'green', trim along the edge with a sharp knife, and so obtain a neat gunwale line again. Leave a little longer, then mix up about $\frac{3}{4}$ lb resin, laminating or gelcoat, and give the whole surface a coating of resin again. Total weight added will be about 4 lbs, but the strength is greatly enhanced. One boat treated in this way is now into its eighth year, two of them with a jacket on.

BROKEN ENDS. Where a canoe has had its end broken off, there is difficulty in lining it up. First, clean off all rough edges, but try and look at it and think about the repair. There are often associated splits and tears in the main part and in the end

179

part. Some of these lend themselves to easy repair through the broken end, and internal repair is easy. The outside is taped over to keep the torn edges in register, and the repairs made internally as far as possible, except those around the gunwale joint, which is probably split anyway. Because the internal joint on the boat is still there it will mask a proper internal repair, and so should not be attempted. Ripping out the internal joint strip is usually a mistake, as it brings further damage in its train.

Having done as much as can be done easily, now tape the end part into place lightly with masking tape. Use half a dozen pieces. Line it up and start to stick it down firmly all over. Leave one part of the joint between end and hull exposed, and laminate a single thickness of 1½-oz mat over the break. Leave it until set. Now remove some of the masking tape on the opposite side of the break, and glass over again, but *not* until the first is set hard enough to carry the weight of the end part. With two tacking joints made, now remove all the tape, and make a glass/resin joint completely all round, externally. Missing areas must be patched as suggested earlier. If you try to make the whole joint at once, you are likely to find it badly distorted, and once it slips, you are in trouble. Take it in three stages and all should be well.

Appendix I

Some tips from a commercial workshop

Recently I was in a commercial grp workshop. The proprietor told me the following:

Keep the working temperature at 65°F (19°C). Keep it constant.

Use Isophthalic resins for making top quality moulds. These are expensive.

Where labour cost is important, then best quality mat is a money saver. Best quality mat is Scandinavian (at present!).

Store resin in cool place under cover. Bring it into the workshop the day before use to warm up.

The ratio of resin to glass should not be more, by weight, than 2:1, and preferably $1\frac{1}{2}$:1. It is possible to get 1:1 with 'Fabmat'.

Two thin gelcoats are far better than one thick one.

When making a mould, lay on one laminate only, allow it to set hard, then lay on other laminations when the first is stabilised, say after three days (this is impossible with amateur building schedules!).

A constant humidity is most important. The air should be dry and warm.

Use the best rollers you can get.

Always use one type of hard roller for consolidating, ribbed, 2″ long, $\frac{3}{4}$″ diameter. It gives the necessary pressure to squeeze the air out. The bigger rollers cover the area quicker but cannot exert the necessary pressure.

181

Appendix II

Sources of materials, moulds, and advice

What will suit you depends on which firm supplies your needs, where you live, what you are prepared to pay, what quality you require, what service you require with it; and so on. The list of firms given here is not exhaustive, but I do know that good service is offered by each one. The identification letters are for easy reference below.

A   Avoncraft, Burrowfield, Welwyn Garden City.
     Tel.: Welwyn Garden City 30000

B   Glaskit, R. C. Laker Ltd, Unit 3, Wessex Road, Bourne End, Bucks. Tel.: Bourne End 25336

C   K. & C. Mouldings Ltd, Shelfanger, Diss, Norfolk

D   Northern Wild Water Centre, The Mill, Glasshouses, Pateley Bridge, via Harrogate, Yorks. Tel.: Pateley Bridge 310 and 624

E   P. & H. Products, 76 Dale Road, Spondon, Derby.
     Tel.: Ilkeston 3155

F   Prima Ltd, Platt's Eyott, Lower Sunbury Road, Hampton-on-Thames, Middlesex. Tel.: 01-979-0164

G   Streamlyte Ltd, Lancing, Sussex. Tel.: Lancing 62431

H   Trylon Ltd, Thrift Street, Wollaston, Wellingborough, Northants. Tel.: Wollaston 275

J   V.C.P. Ltd, Woodley Street, Ruddington, Nottingham.
     Tel.: 0602-214092
     Tools from B and C particularly, but all supply.
     Materials from all the above.

Sources of materials, moulds and advice

Moulds from A, D, E, F, G, H and J.
Advice on canoeing matters from all except C.
Booklets on canoe building from F, G, and H.
Courses are arranged by H, but all welcome visits, given prior notice. They are all busy working workshops as well as supplying materials.

Bibliography

The books I have found useful on design are as follows:
Surf and Sea by J. M. Kelly Jr (Barnes, New York). Very good on surfboard design and planing hull shape.
Sail Theory and Practice by C. A. Marchaj (Adlard Coles). General information about sailing hulls, with some reference to rudders, keels, wake formations, and a reference to IC 10, the International sailing canoe.
Skene's Elements of Yacht Design by F. S. Kinney (A & C Black). Good on practical yacht design and how to calculate quantities. Some insight into small hulls.
Rushton and his Times in American Canoeing by Attwood Manley (Syracuse University Press/Adirondack Museum). Excellent drawings of late nineteenth-century canoes and kayaks, plus many beautiful photographs of the true traditional Canadian canoes.
The Bark Canoes and the Skin Boats of North America (Bulletin 230, Smithsonian Institute, Washington). The definitive work on kayak and Canadian canoe outlines, and constructional details.
British Coracles and Irish Curraghs by James Hornell (Society for Nautical Research, National Maritime Museum, Greenwich). The definitive work on native British light craft, with many outline drawings and photographs.
The books which I have used to derive much of the technical information on grp work are as follows:

184

Bibliography

Complete Amateur Boat Builder by Michael Verney (John Murray). Dated now, but sound enough. It was the first book I had on grp work on which there is one chapter. The rest of the book is good on alternative methods of construction of small hulls.

Polyester Handbook (Scott Bader, Wollaston, Wellingborough, Northants). Excellent book with fine drawings and photographs and many technical details on resin performance, and some casting faults.

Cellobond Polyester Resins (Technical Manual no. 12. British Resin Products). Very good on grp methods in industry.

How to Build a Glass Fibre Canoe (Trylon, Wollaston, Wellingborough, Northants). Booklet on canoe building in grp. Very good basic work. But if you have read this far, you have covered what is in that book.

Canoeing Complete by Skilling (Nicholas Kaye). Chapter on canoe building, written just before this book was started, by Alan Byde.

Living Canoeing by Alan W Byde (A & C Black). Chapter on canoe building out of which this work has grown. Good all-round book on the sport of canoeing.

The Beginner's Guide to Canoeing by Alan W. Byde (Pelham). Basic canoeing book with several canoeing stories. Contains very little about grp.

Index

186

Index